JavaScript and JSON Essentials

Second Edition

Build light weight, scalable, and faster web applications with the power of JSON

Bruno Joseph D'mello
Sai Srinivas Sriparasa

BIRMINGHAM - MUMBAI

JavaScript and JSON Essentials
Second Edition

Commissioning Editor: Amarabha Banerjee
Acquisition Editor: Noyonika Das
Content Development Editor: Gauri Pradhan
Technical Editor: Shweta Jadhav
Copy Editor: Safis Editing
Project Coordinator: Sheejal Shah
Proofreader: Safis Editing
Indexer: Priyanka Dhadke
Graphics: Jason Monteiro
Production Coordinator: Nilesh Mohite

First published: October 2013
Second edition: April 2018

Production reference: 1170418

Published by Packt Publishing Ltd.
Livery Place
35 Livery Street
Birmingham
B3 2PB, UK.

ISBN 978-1-78862-470-1

www.packtpub.com

To my father, Joseph Victor Dmello, for exemplifying the power of commitment rather than attachment of failures and for always being an inspiration.

– Bruno Joseph Dmello

`mapt.io`

Mapt is an online digital library that gives you full access to over 5,000 books and videos, as well as industry leading tools to help you plan your personal development and advance your career. For more information, please visit our website.

Why subscribe?

- Spend less time learning and more time coding with practical eBooks and Videos from over 4,000 industry professionals

- Improve your learning with Skill Plans built especially for you

- Get a free eBook or video every month

- Mapt is fully searchable

- Copy and paste, print, and bookmark content

PacktPub.com

Did you know that Packt offers eBook versions of every book published, with PDF and ePub files available? You can upgrade to the eBook version at `www.PacktPub.com` and as a print book customer, you are entitled to a discount on the eBook copy. Get in touch with us at `service@packtpub.com` for more details.

At `www.PacktPub.com`, you can also read a collection of free technical articles, sign up for a range of free newsletters, and receive exclusive discounts and offers on Packt books and eBooks.

Contributors

About the authors

Bruno Joseph D'mello is a proactive software engineer at yapsody. He is a JavaScript enthusiast and loves working with open source communities. He possesses around 6 years of experience in software development, of which 4 years were dedicated to working on JS technologies. Bruno follows kaizen and enjoys the freedom of architecting new things. He is socially active via coaching web technologies or participating in other research projects and meetups. When not coding, Bruno likes to spend time with his guitar, family, and friends.

Special thanks to the overall Packt Publishing team, which was working hard in the background and making this book a success (especially Gauri Pradhan for her perfect coordination), and also the reviewer team, Erina Rodrigues and Fazal Momin, for their brainy and valuable input.

Sai Srinivas Sriparasa is a web developer and an open source evangelist living in the Stamford area. Sai was the lead developer involved in building the Dr. Ozs website and has led teams for companies such as Sprint Nextel, West Interactive, and Apple. Sai's repertoire includes JavaScript, PHP, Python, HTML5, responsive web development, ASP.NET, C#, and Silverlight.

About the reviewers

Erina is completing her master's and proactively working as an assistant professor in the computer science department of Thakur college, Mumbai. Her enthusiasm in web technologies inspires her to contribute for freelance JavaScript projects, especially on node.js. Her research topics were SDN and IoT, which according to her create amazing solutions for various web technologies when they are used together. Nowadays, she focuses on blockchain and enjoys fiddling with its concepts in JavaScript.

I would like to sincerely thank the Packt Publishing team for providing an opportunity as a reviewer, and also acknowledge my family for their support and love.

Fazal Momin was born on 25th December 1992 in Mumbai, pursued his formal education and received his bachelor's degree in engineering in the field of information technology in 2014. During his second year of engineering, in 2012, he pursued a certification to help him learn web technologies and then started his career as a coach in web technologies. In 2014, he started working with an e-commerce service provider company as a software developer in the field of web development and data science. In 2017, he transitioned to the role of a backend developer for a robotics company in Mumbai.

Thank you Bruno Dmello for asking and providing me the opportunity to review JavaScript and JSON Essentials, Second Edition. This is a great book; I personally have learned a lot while reviewing it. Many thanks to Sheejal Shah for being there to help me keep the deliverables on track. Thank you to all the people at Packt Publishing for publishing this wonderful book.

Packt is searching for authors like you

If you're interested in becoming an author for Packt, please visit `authors.packtpub.com` and apply today. We have worked with thousands of developers and tech professionals, just like you, to help them share their insight with the global tech community. You can make a general application, apply for a specific hot topic that we are recruiting an author for, or submit your own idea.

Table of Contents

Preface

JSON is an established standard format used to exchange data. This book shows how JSON plays different roles in full web development using various examples. By the end of this book, you'll have a new perspective on providing solutions to your applications and handling complexity.

Who this book is for

If you're a web developer with a basic understanding of JavaScript or PHP development and wish to write JSON data and integrate it with RESTful APIs to create faster and scalable applications, this book is for you.

What this book covers

Chapter 1, *Getting Started with JSON*, introduces the audience to JSON, discusses the history of JSON along with how it works and stores itself in memory. The chapter also outlines the popular programming languages that support JSON and ends by writing a basic program with different data types in JSON.

Chapter 2, *The JSON Structures*, spices up the normal implementation of JSON with a little complexity consisting of multiple datatypes, multiple objects, and multidimensional data.

Chapter 3, *AJAX Requests with JSON*, discusses AJAX requests with JSON data, passing JSON over HTTP requests, asynchronicity and techniques to handle it.

Chapter 4, *Cross-Domain Asynchronous Requests*, explores the concept of making asynchronous calls across domains. Since data is being transported across domains, users will be introduced to the concept of JSON with padding, called JSONP.

Chapter 5, *Debugging JSON*, explains the powerful tools that are available to debug, validate, and format JSON.

Chapter 6, *Building the Carousel Application*, implements the idea of a Carousel application and the required setup and dependencies, such as the jQuery library and the jQuery Cycle plugin, for the application. It uses Bootstrap to maintain a basic design for the application.

`Chapter 7`, *Alternate Implementations of JSON*, discusses the non web-development implementation of JSON, such as dependency managers, metadata stores, and configuration stores.

`Chapter 8`, *Introduction to Hapi.js*, talks about implementing JSON-based configuration in a Hapi server and creating RESTful APIs with the help of the same.

`Chapter 9`, *Storing JSON Documents in MongoDB*, begins by introducing MongoDB and then, explains how JSON is used in mongoDB. Next, it reaches the central theme of performing different operations on mongoDB JSON documents.

`Chapter 10`, *Configuring the Task Runner Using JSON*, outlines the gulp.js library. Gulp is a powerful library that manages and provides tools to create tasks.

`Chapter 11`, *JSON for Real-Time and Distributed Data*, familiarizes you with the usage of JSON data for real-time web applications by implementing the socket.io server and, furthermore, with Apache Kafka.

`Chapter 12`, *Case Studies in JSON*, is a case study on how JSON is enhanced for different domains, taking into consideration the various benefits it provided after implantation.

To get the most out of this book

1. If you are a beginner in web development, start with `chapter 1`, *Getting Started with JSON*, and go through the basics of JSON. The first five chapters are simple to understand and quick to practice. As you move forward, go on implementing the snippets that are provided in each chapter.
2. Over time, ensure that all your book-related queries are solved by discussing them on forums such as StackOverflow or GitHub.

Download the example code files

You can download the example code files for this book from your account at `www.packtpub.com`. If you purchased this book elsewhere, you can visit `www.packtpub.com/support` and register to have the files emailed directly to you.

You can download the code files by following these steps:

1. Log in or register at `www.packtpub.com`.
2. Select the **SUPPORT** tab.
3. Click on **Code Downloads & Errata**.
4. Enter the name of the book in the **Search** box and follow the onscreen instructions.

Once the file is downloaded, please make sure that you unzip or extract the folder using the latest version of:

- WinRAR/7-Zip for Windows
- Zipeg/iZip/UnRarX for Mac
- 7-Zip/PeaZip for Linux

The code bundle for the book is also hosted on GitHub at `https://github.com/PacktPublishing/JavaScript-and-JSON-Essentials-Second-Edition`. In case there's an update to the code, it will be updated on the existing GitHub repository.

We also have other code bundles from our rich catalog of books and videos available at `https://github.com/PacktPublishing/`. Check them out!

Download the color images

We also provide a PDF file that has color images of the screenshots/diagrams used in this book. You can download it here: `http://www.packtpub.com/sites/default/files/downloads/JavaScriptandJSONEssentialsSecondEdition_ColorImages.pdf`.

Conventions used

There are a number of text conventions used throughout this book.

`CodeInText`: Indicates code words in text, database table names, folder names, filenames, file extensions, pathnames, dummy URLs, user input, and Twitter handles. Here is an example: "Mount the downloaded `WebStorm-10*.dmg` disk image file as another disk in your system."

A block of code is set as follows:

```
for(let j=0;j<designationCount;j++){
    designations+= `, ${data_json[i].designation.title[j]}`;
}
```

When we wish to draw your attention to a particular part of a code block, the relevant lines or items are set in bold:

```
const http = require('http');
const port = 3300;
http.createServer((req, res) => {
    res.writeHead(200, {
      "Content-Type": "application/json"
    });
    res.write(JSON.stringify({
      greet : "Hello Readers!"
    }));
    res.end();
}).listen(port);
console.log(`Node Server is running on port : ${port}`)
```

Any command-line input or output is written as follows:

```
$ mkdir test-node-app
$ cd test-node-app
$ npm init
```

Bold: Indicates a new term, an important word, or words that you see onscreen. For example, words in menus or dialog boxes appear in the text like this. Here is an example: "Select **System info** from the **Administration** panel."

Warnings or important notes appear like this.

Tips and tricks appear like this.

Get in touch

Feedback from our readers is always welcome.

General feedback: Email `feedback@packtpub.com` and mention the book title in the subject of your message. If you have questions about any aspect of this book, please email us at `questions@packtpub.com`.

Errata: Although we have taken every care to ensure the accuracy of our content, mistakes do happen. If you have found a mistake in this book, we would be grateful if you would report this to us. Please visit `www.packtpub.com/submit-errata`, selecting your book, clicking on the Errata Submission Form link, and entering the details.

Piracy: If you come across any illegal copies of our works in any form on the Internet, we would be grateful if you would provide us with the location address or website name. Please contact us at `copyright@packtpub.com` with a link to the material.

If you are interested in becoming an author: If there is a topic that you have expertise in and you are interested in either writing or contributing to a book, please visit `authors.packtpub.com`.

Reviews

Please leave a review. Once you have read and used this book, why not leave a review on the site that you purchased it from? Potential readers can then see and use your unbiased opinion to make purchase decisions, we at Packt can understand what you think about our products, and our authors can see your feedback on their book. Thank you!

For more information about Packt, please visit `packtpub.com`.

Getting Started with JSON 1

JSON (**JavaScript Object Notation**) is a very popular data interchange format. It was discovered by Sir Douglas Crockford. According to Douglas, JSON always existed in terms of object notation, so he didn't invent it. He was the first person to provide the specifications and engineer JSON so that it can be used as a standardized format.

In this chapter, we are going to cover the following topics:

- What JSON is
- How JSON is implemented using a simple Hello World program
- How JSON is stored in memory
- Datatypes in JSON
- Various languages that support JSON
- PHP and Python explained in brief

Now for all the beginners, who have just heard the term JSON for the first time, the following section helps to visualize it in detail.

JSON, a data exchange format

To define **JSON**, we can say it is a text-based, lightweight, and human-readable format for data exchange between clients and servers. JSON is derived from JavaScript and bears a close resemblance to JavaScript objects, but it is not dependent on JavaScript. JSON is language-independent, and support for the JSON data format is available in all popular languages, some of which are C#, PHP, Java, C++, Python, and Ruby.

JSON can be used in web applications for data transfer. Consider the following block diagram of the simple client-server architecture. Assume that the client is a browser that sends an HTTP request to the server, and the server serves the request and responses as expected. This is visualized as in the following screenshot:

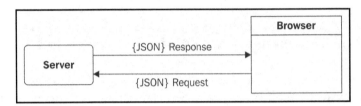

In the preceding two-way communication, the data format used is a serialized string, with the combination of key-value pairs enveloped in parentheses; that is JSON!

Prior to JSON, XML was considered to be the chosen data interchange format. XML parsing required an XML DOM implementation on the client side that would ingest the XML response, and then XPath was used to query the response in order to access and retrieve the data. This made life tedious, as querying for data had to be performed at two levels: first on the server side where the data was being queried from a database, and a second time on the client side using XPath. JSON does not need any specific implementations; the JavaScript engine in the browser handles JSON parsing.

XML messages often tend to be heavy and verbose and take up a lot of bandwidth while sending the data over a network connection. Once the XML message is retrieved, it has to be loaded into memory to parse it; let us take a look at a `students` data feed in XML and JSON.

The following is an example in XML:

```xml
<?xml version="1.0" encoding="UTF-8" ?>
<!-- This is an example of student feed in XML -->
<students>
  <student>
    <studentid>101</studentid>
    <firstname>John</firstname>
    <lastname>Doe</lastname>
    <classes>
      <class>Business Research</class>
      <class>Economics</class>
      <class>Finance</class>
    </classes>
  </student>
  <student>
```

```
      <studentid>102</studentid>
      <firstname>Jane</firstname>
      <lastname>Dane</lastname>
      <classes>
        <class>Marketing</class>
        <class>Economics</class>
        <class>Finance</class>
      </classes>
    </student>
  </students>
```

Let us take a look at the example in JSON:

```
/* This is an example of student feed in JSON */
{
  "students" :{
    "0" :{
      "studentid" : 101,
      "firstname" : "John",
      "lastname" : "Doe",
      "classes" : [
        "Business Research",
        "Economics",
        "Finance"
      ]
    },
    "1" :{
      "studentid" : 102,
      "firstname" : "Jane",
      "lastname" : "Dane",
      "classes" : [
        "Marketing",
        "Economics",
        "Finance"
      ]
    }
  }
}
```

As we notice, the size of the XML message is bigger when compared to its JSON counterpart, and this is just for two records. A real-time feed will begin with a few thousand and go upwards. Another point to note is that the amount of data that has to be generated by the server and then transmitted over the internet is already big, and XML, as it is verbose, makes it bigger. Given that we are in the age of mobile devices where smartphones and tablets are getting more and more popular by the day, transmitting such large volumes of data on a slower network causes slow page loads, hang-ups, and poor user experience, thus driving users away from the site. JSON has come to be the preferred internet data interchange format, to avoid the issues mentioned earlier. Since JSON is used to transmit serialized data over the internet, we will need to make a note of its MIME type.

Let us zoom in on the following block diagram, which shows how the requested data is sent in the client-server architecture mentioned earlier:

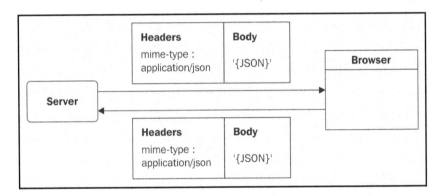

A **Multipurpose Internet Mail Extensions** (**MIME**) type is an internet media type; it is a two-part identifier for content that is being transferred over the internet. MIME types are passed through the HTTP headers of an HTTP Request and an HTTP Response. The MIME type is the communication of content type between the server and the browser. In general, a MIME type will have two or more parts that give the browser information about the type of data that is being sent either in the HTTP Request or in the HTTP Response. The MIME type for JSON data is **application/json**. If MIME type headers are not sent across the browser, it treats the incoming JSON as plain text.

Nowadays, the `content-type` key, which is derived from `mime-type` itself, is used in the headers.

The Hello World program with JSON

Now that we have a basic understanding of JSON, let us work on our Hello World program. This is shown in the snippet that follows:

```
<!DOCTYPE html>
<html>
  <head>
    <title>Test Javascript</title>
    <script type="text/javascript">
      let hello_world = {"Hello":"World"};
      alert(hello_world.Hello);
    </script>
  </head>
  <body>
    <h2>JSON Hello World</h2>
    <p>This is a test program to alert Hello world!</p>
  </body>
</html>
```

The preceding program will display **Hello World** on the screen when it is invoked from a browser.

 We are using `let`, which is a new ecmascript identifier. It differs from the normal variable declaration identifier, `var`, with respect to scoping. The former is scoped to the nearest function block while the latter is scoped to the nearest enclosing block. For more details please refer to the following URL: `https://developer.mozilla.org/en-US/docs/Web/JavaScript/Reference/Statements/let`.

Let us pay close attention to the script between the `<script>` tags:

```
let hello_world = {"Hello":"World"};
alert(hello_world.Hello);
```

In the first step, we are creating a JavaScript variable and initializing the variable with a JavaScript object. Similar to how we retrieve data from a JavaScript object, we use the key-value pair to retrieve the value. Simply put, JSON is a collection of key and value pairs, where every key is a reference to the memory location where the value is stored on the computer. Now let us take a step back and analyse why we need JSON if all we are doing is assigning JavaScript objects that are readily available. The answer is, JSON is a different format altogether, unlike JavaScript, which is a language.

 JSON keys and values have to be enclosed in double quotes. If either is enclosed in single quotes, we will receive an error.

Now, let us take a quick look at the similarities and differences between JSON and a normal JavaScript object. If we were to create a similar JavaScript object like our `hello_world` JSON variable from the earlier example, it would look like the JavaScript object that follows:

```
let hello_world = {"Hello":"World"};
```

The big difference here is that the key is not wrapped in double quotes. Since JSON key is a string, we can use any valid string for a key. We can use spaces, special characters, and hyphens in our keys, none of which are valid in a normal JavaScript object:

```
let hello_world = {"test-hello":"World"};
```

When we use special characters, hyphens, or spaces in our keys, we have to be careful while accessing them:

```
alert(hello_world.test-hello); //doesn't work
```

The reason the preceding JavaScript statement doesn't work is that JavaScript doesn't accept keys with special characters, hyphens, or strings. So, we have to retrieve the data using a method where we will handle the JSON object as an associative array with a string key. This is shown in the snippet that follows:

```
alert(hello_world["test-hello"]); //Hurray! It work
```

Another difference between the two is that a JavaScript object can carry functions within, while JSON object cannot carry any functions. The example that follows has the property `getFullName`, which has a function that alerts the name `John Doe` when it is invoked:

```
{
    "studentid" : 101,
    "firstname" : "John",
    "lastname" : "Doe",
```

```
    "isStudent" : true,
    "classes" : [
      "Business Research",
      "Economics",
      "Finance"
    ],
    "getFullName" : function(){
      alert(`${this.firstname} ${this.lastname}`);
    }
}
```

 Note that the string interpolation feature is a new ES feature that can be used when writing variables and functions inside the expression `${}`. The expression only works in tilde inverted commas and not in other types of inverted commas.

Finally, the biggest difference is that a JavaScript object was never intended to be a data interchange format, while the sole purpose of JSON was to act as a data interchange format.

In the upcoming section, we are going to learn about JSON memory allocation.

How is JSON stored in memory?

In following example, a discussion of JSON compared to a JavaScript object, we arrive at the conclusion that JSON is nothing more than a stringified representation of the object. To understand its storage procedure conceptually, consider the following example:

```
let completeJSON = {
    "hello": "World is a great place",
    "num": 5
}
```

Let us divide this concept with respect to the major operations that are performed on a complete JSON. When I say complete JSON, I mean the whole structure and not its subset of key-value pairs. So the first operation is to *serialize*. **Serialization** is the process of removing blank spaces as well as escaping the internal inverted quotes (if any) so as to convert the whole structure into a single string. This can be illustrated as follows:

```
let stringifiedJSON = JSON.stringify(completeJSON);
```

If you `console.log` the variable `stringifiedJSON`, we get the following output:

```
"{"hello":"World is a great place","num":5}"
```

In this case, the whole JSON is stored as a normal string. Let's represent it as follows:

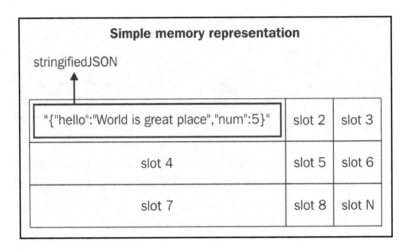

In the preceding conceptual block diagram, slot 1 of the memory location is represented by `stringifiedJSON` with a single input string value. The next type of storage might be parsed JSON. By using the previous snippet, if we parse the `stringifiedJSON` we get the output as follows:

```
let parsedJSON = JSON.parse(stringifiedJSON);
```

The output received will be :

```
{
    "hello": "World is a great place",
    "num": 5
}
```

In the preceding representation of JSON, it is clearly identified that the value received is not a string but an object; to be more precise, it is a JavaScript object notation. Now, the notion of storage of JSON in memory is the same as the JavaScript object.

Assume that we are using a JavaScript engine to interpret code.

Hence, in this case, the scenario is totally different. Let us visualize it as follows:

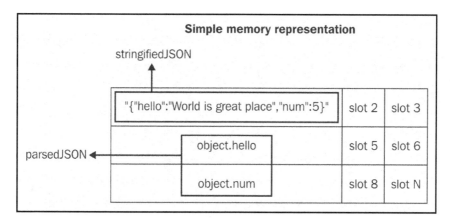

Now, let us derive some inferences after observing the memory representation:

- Object storage is not sequential; the memory slots are randomly selected. In our case it's slots 4 and 7.
- The data stored in each slot is a reference to the different memory location. Let us call it an address.

So, considering our example, we have the fourth slot with the address `object.hello`. Now, this address is pointing to a different memory location. Assume that the location is the third slot, which is handled by the JavaScript execution context. Thus, the value of `parsedJSON.hello` is held by the third slot.

Datatypes in JSON

Now, let us take a look at a more complex example of JSON. We'll also go over all the datatypes that are supported by JSON. JSON supports six data types: strings, numbers, Booleans, arrays, objects, and null:

```
{
    "studentid" : 101,
    "firstname" : "John",
```

```
    "lastname" : "Doe",
    "isStudent" : true,
    "scores" : [40, 50],
    "courses" : {
        "major" : "Finance",
        "minor" : "Marketing"
    }
}
```

In the preceding example, we have key-value pairs of different data types. Now let us take a close look at each of these key-value pairs.

The datatype of the value that "studentid" references is a number:

```
"studentid" : 101,
```

The datatype of the value that "firstname" references is a string:

```
"firstname" : "John",
```

In the following snippet, the datatype of the value that "isStudent" references is a Boolean:

```
"isStudent" : true,
```

The datatype of the value that "scores" references here is an array:

```
"scores" : [40, 50]
```

The datatype of the value that "courses" references is an object:

```
"courses" : {
    "major" : "Finance",
    "minor" : "Marketing"
}
```

We know that JSON supports six datatypes; they are strings, numbers, Booleans, arrays, objects, and null. Yes, JSON supports null data, and real-time business implementations need accurate information. There might be cases where null was substituted with an empty string, but that is inaccurate. Let us take a quick look at the following example:

```
let nullVal = "";
alert(typeof nullVal); //prints string
nullVal = null;
alert(typeof nullVal); //prints object
```

Arrays and null values are objects in JavaScript.

In the preceding example, we are performing some simple operations such as determining the type of an empty string. We are using the `typeof` operator that takes an operand and returns the datatype of that operand, while on the next line we are determining the type of a null value.

Now, let us implement our JSON object in a page and retrieve the values, as shown in the following snippet:

```
<!DOCTYPE html>
<html>
<head>
  <script type="text/javascript">
    let complexJson = {
        "studentid" : 101,
        "firstname" : "John",
        "lastname" : "Doe",
        "isStudent" : true,
        "scores" : [40, 50],
        "courses" : {
            "major" : "Finance",
            "minor" : "Marketing"
        }
    };
  </script>
</head>
<body>
  <h2>Complex Data in JSON</h2>
  <p>This is a test program to load complex json data into a variable</p>
</body>
</html>
```

To retrieve the `id` from the variable `complexJson`, we need to do the following:

```
alert(complexJson.studentid); //101
```

To retrieve the `name` from the variable `complexJson`, look at the following snippet:

```
alert(complexJson.firstname); //John
```

Look at the following code to retrieve `isStudent` from the variable `complexJson`:

```
alert(complexJson.isStudent); //true
```

Retrieving data from arrays and objects gets a little tricky, as we have to traverse through the array or object. Let us see how values can be retrieved from arrays:

```
alert(complexJson.scores[1]); //50
```

In the preceding example, we are retrieving the second element (with index 1, as the array starts from 0) from the `scores` array. Although `scores` is an array inside the `complexJson` object, it is still treated as a regular key-value pair. It is handled differently when the key is accessed; the first thing that the interpreter has to assess when a key is accessed is how to get the datatype of its value. If the retrieved value is a string, number, Boolean, or null, there will be no extra operations performed on the value. But if it is an array or an object, the value's dependencies are taken into consideration.

To retrieve an element from the object inside JSON object, we will have to access the key that is the reference for that value, as shown:

```
alert(complexJson.courses.major); //Finance
```

Since objects do not have a numeric index, JavaScript might rearrange the order of items inside an object. If you notice that the order of key-value pairs during the initialization of the JSON object is different from when you are accessing the data, there is nothing to worry about. There is no loss of data; the JavaScript engine has just reordered your object.

Languages that support JSON

Until now, we have seen how parsers in JavaScript support JSON. There are many other programming languages that provide implementations for JSON. Languages such as PHP, Python, C#, C++, and Java provide very good support for the JSON data interchange format. All of the popular programming languages that support service-oriented architectures understand the importance of JSON and its implementation for data transfer, and thus have provided great support for JSON. Let us take a quick detour from implementing JSON in JavaScript, and see how JSON is implemented in other languages, such as PHP and Python.

JSON implementation in PHP

PHP is considered to be one of the most popular languages for building web applications. It is a server-side scripting language and allows developers to build applications that can perform operations on the server, connect to a database to perform **CRUD** (**Create, Read, Update, Delete**) operations, and provide a stately environment for real-time applications. JSON support has been built into the PHP core from PHP 5.2.0; this helps users avoid going through any complex installations or configurations. Given that JSON is just a data interchange format, PHP consists of two functions. These functions handle JSON that comes in via a request or generate JSON that will be sent via a response. PHP is a weakly-typed language; for this example, we will use the data stored in a PHP array and convert that data into JSON string, which can be utilized as a data feed. Let us recreate the student example that we used in an earlier section, build it in PHP, and convert it into JSON:

This example is only intended to show you how JSON can be generated using PHP.

```php
<?php
  $student = array(
    "id"=>101,
    "name"=>"John Doe",
    "isStudent"=>true,
    "scores"=>array(40, 50);
    "courses"=>array(
      "major"=>"Finance",
      "minor"=>"Marketing"
    );
  );

  //Echo is used to print the data
  echo json_encode($student); //encoding the array into JSON string

?>
```

To run a PHP script, we will need to install PHP. To run a PHP script through a browser, we will need a web server, such as Apache or IIS. We will go through the installation in Chapter 3, *AJAX Requests with JSON*, when we work with AJAX.

This script starts by initializing a variable and assigning an associative array that contains student information. The variable $students is then passed to a function called json_encode(), which converts the variable into JSON string. When this script is run, it generates a valid response that can be exposed as JSON data feed for other applications to utilize.

The output is as follows:

```
{
    "id": 101,
    "name": "John Doe",
    "isStudent": true,
    "scores": [40, 50],
    "courses":
    {
        "major": "Finance",
        "minor": "Marketing"
    }
}
```

We have successfully generated our first JSON feed via a simple PHP script; let us take a look at the method to parse JSON that comes in via an HTTP request. It is common for web applications that make asynchronous HTTP requests to send data in JSON format:

 This example is only intended to show you how JSON can be ingested into PHP.

```
$student = '{"id":101,"name":"John
Doe","isStudent":true,"scores":[40,50],"courses":{"major":"Finance","minor"
:"Marketing"}}';
//Decoding JSON string into php array
print_r(json_decode($student));
```

The output is as follows:

```
Object(
  [id] => 101
  [name] => John Doe
  [isStudent] => 1
  [scores] => Array([0] => 40[1] => 50)
  [courses] => stdClass
  Object([major] => Finance[minor] => Marketing)
)
```

JSON implementation in Python

Python is a very popular scripting language that is extensively used to perform string operations and to build console applications. It can be used to fetch data from JSON API, and once the JSON data is retrieved it will be treated as JSON string. To perform any operations on that JSON string, Python provides the JSON module. The JSON module is an amalgamation of many powerful functions that we can use to parse the JSON string on hand:

This example is only intended to show you how JSON can be generated using Python.

```
import json

student = [{
    "studentid" : 101,
    "firstname" : "John",
    "lastname" : "Doe",
## make sure we have first letter capitalize in case of boolean
    "isStudent" : True,
    "scores" : [40, 50],
    "courses" : {
        "major" : "Finance",
        "minor" : "Marketing"
    }
}]

print json.dumps(student)
```

In this example we have used complex datatypes, such as Tuples and Dictionaries, to store the scores and courses respectively; since this is not a Python course, we will not go into those datatypes in any depth.

To run this script, Python2 needs to be installed. It comes preinstalled on any *nix operating system. Play with our code in Python with the following online executor: https://www.jdoodle.com/python-programming-online.

The output is as follows:

```
[{"studentid": 101, "firstname": "John", "lastname": "Doe", "isStudent":
true, "courses": {"major": "Finance", "minor": "Marketing"}, "scores": [40,
50]}]
```

The keys might get rearranged based on the datatype; we can use the sort_keys flag to retrieve the original order.

Now, let us take a quick look at how the JSON decoding is performed in Python:

 This example is only intended to show you how JSON can be ingested into Python.

```
student_json = '''[{"studentid": 101, "firstname": "John", "lastname":
"Doe", "isStudent": true, "courses": {"major": "Finance", "minor":
"Marketing"}, "scores": [40, 50]}]'''

print json.loads(student_json)
```

In this example, we are storing the JSON string in student_json, and we are using the json.loads() method that is available through the JSON module in Python.

The output is as follows:

```
[
{
    u 'studentid': 101,
    u 'firstname': u 'John',
    u 'lastname': u 'Doe',
    u 'isStudent': True,
    u 'courses':
    {
        u 'major': u 'Finance',
        u 'minor': u 'Marketing'
    },
    u 'scores': [40, 50]
}]
```

Summary

This chapter introduced us to the basics of JSON. We went through the history of JSON and understood its advantages over XML. We created our first JSON object and successfully parsed it. Also, we went over all the datatypes that JSON supports. Finally, we went over some examples as to how JSON can be implemented in other programming languages. As we move forward in this journey, we will find the knowledge that we have gathered in this chapter to be a solid foundation for more complex concepts such as accessing multilevel JSON and performing data storage operations on them, which we will be looking at in later chapters.

2
The JSON Structures

In Chapter 1, *Getting Started with JSON*, you were introduced to basic JSON, how JSON objects can be embedded into an HTML file, and how basic operations such as accessing keys can be performed on simple JSON objects. Now it's time to move ahead with some simple yet advanced steps. In this chapter, you will learn about:

- Inserting external JavaScript
- Accessing multilevel JSON objects
- Performing modifications in JSON data

Now let's take a step forward and work with JSON objects that are bigger, more complex, and closer to the JSON that we would work with in real-world situations.

Inserting external JavaScript

In real-world applications, JSON can be retrieved either as a response from an asynchronous request or from a JSON feed. A website uses HTML, CSS, and JavaScript to provide a visually beautiful user interface. But there are cases where data vendors are only focused on getting data. A data feed serves their purpose; a feed is a crude way of supplying data so that others can reuse it to display the data on their websites or to ingest the data and run their algorithms on it. Such data feeds are big and cannot be directly embedded into the script tag. Let us look at how external JavaScript files can be included in an HTML file.

The following screenshot depicts the code for the `external-js.html` file:

```html
<!DOCTYPE html>
<html>
<head>
  <title>Include external javascript</title>
  <script type="text/javascript" src="example.js"></script>
  <script type="text/javascript">
    alert(x);
  </script>
</head>
<body>
  <h2>Include external javascript</h2>
  <p>This is a test program to learn how external javascript files can be
included</p>
</body>
</html>
```

In this example, we include `example.js`, which is an external JavaScript file:

```
const x = "This is value of x and is being retrieved from external js
file";
```

 Note that the `const` keyword is used as a variable identifier for representing immutable data. Once declared, the constant x cannot be reassigned. For more details see the following link: `https://developer.mozilla.org/en-US/docs/Web/JavaScript/Reference/Statements/const`.

To access the constant x that is in the `example.js` file from the `external-js.html` file, we write our programs within our script tags in the HTML file.

This file has to be created in the same folder as `external-js.html`. Follow the given folder structure:

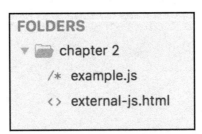

Accessing objects in JSON

Now that we understand how to make a script call to fetch an external JavaScript file, let us use the same technique to import a JSON feed. I have generated a test `employee` JSON data feed with 100 records. To traverse through any JSON feed, it is important to make a note of how the data is arranged. The keys in this data feed are basic employee information such as employee number, date of birth, first name, last name, gender, hire date, titles that they have held, and the dates during which they have held those titles. A few employees have held the same title throughout their tenure, while there are some employees who have held more than one title.

 This JSON file will be part of the code files for exercises.

Consider the following JSON store that we need to use to perform the operations:

```
let data_json = [
  {
    "emp_no" : "10001",
    "birth_date" : "1980-09-02",
    "first_name" : "Georgi",
    "last_name" : "Facello",
    "gender" : "M",
    "hire_date" : "2010-09-04",
    "designation" : {
      "title" : "Junior Engineer",
      "From_date" : "2010-09-04",
      "to_date" : "2017-10-11"
    }
  },
  {
    "emp_no" : "10002",
    "birth_date" : "1970-09-02",
    "first_name" : "Will",
    "last_name" : "Scott",
    "gender" : "M",
    "hire_date" : "2005-09-04",
    "designation" : {
      "title"   : ["Senior Engineer", "Author", "Trainer"],
      "From_date" : "2005-09-04",
      "to_date" : "2017-10-11"
    }
  },
```

```
{
  "emp_no" : "10003",
  "birth_date" : "1960-09-02",
  "first_name" : "Jenny",
  "last_name" : "Souza",
  "gender" : "F",
  "hire_date" : "2006-10-05",
  "designation" : {
    "title" : "Architect",
    "From_date" : "2006-10-05",
    "to_date" : "2017-10-11"
  }
}
// And so on
]
```

As we are dealing with a complex JSON data feed, let us save the data feed to a file. In the `data_json_feed.html` file, we have imported the `data.json` file, which is in the same folder as the HTML file. It is noteworthy that the JSON feed has been assigned to a variable called `data_json`, and to access the JSON feed, we will have to use this variable in the `data_json_feed.html` file:

```html
<!DOCTYPE html>
<html>
  <head>
    <title>Test Javascript</title>
    <script type="text/javascript" src="data.js"></script>
    <script type="text/javascript">
      console.log(data_json);
    </script>
  </head>
  <body>
    <h2>Include External JSON</h2>
    <p>This is a test program to Learn How external JSON
      feed stored in files can be included.
    </p>
  </body>
</html>
```

Another thing to note is the use of a new method called `console.log`. Browsers such as Mozilla Firefox, Google Chrome, and Apple Safari profile a **Console** panel for run-time JavaScript development and debugging. The use of the JavaScript function alert is discouraged due to its obtrusive behavior. `console.log`, on the other hand, is unobtrusive and logs its messages to the **Console** panel. From here on, we will refrain from using the `alert` method and will use `console.log` to print data into the **Console** window. Google Chrome and Apple Safari come with developer tools already installed; to view the **Console**, right-click on the page and click on **Inspect Element**. Both of them come with a **Console** tab that allows us to work with our logging. Firefox is dependent on Firebug; in `Chapter 5, Debugging JSON`, I will walk you through the installation steps for Firebug:

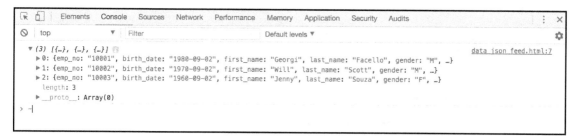

When we load the `data_json_feed.html` file into the Firefox browser, open up our **Console** window, and click on the **DOM** tab, we are going to see a list of 100 `employee` objects. If our object is small and has one or two child objects, we would prefer using their numeric indexes to access them; in this case, as we have a huge number of child objects, it is not realistic to target objects based on static indexes. To illustrate this statement consider the following example:

```
/** Not realistic, unless we are targeting a specific key.**/
Ex : console.log(employees[1].emp_no);
```

Performing complex operations

To tackle an array of objects, we have to handle them in an iterative method. We will have to come up with an iterative solution in which we target one object at a time; once the object is accessed, we will not target that object again. This allows us to maintain data integrity as we can avoid accessing the same object multiple times, thereby avoiding any redundancies. The looping statements in JavaScript are the `while` loop and the `for` loop. Let us take a quick look at how we can use these looping techniques to traverse through our employee's array:

```html
<!DOCTYPE html>
<html>
  <head>
    <title>Test Javascript</title>
    <script type="text/javascript" src="data.js"></script>
    <script type="text/javascript">
      console.log(data_json);
      const employeeCount = data_json.length;
      for(let i=0;i<employeeCount;i++){
        console.log("Employee number is ", data_json[i].emp_no);
      }
    </script>
  </head>
  <body>
    <h2>Parse JSON Feed using While</h2>
    <p>This is a test program to learn how external JSON
      feed stored in files can be parsed using the for Loop.</p>
    </p>
  </body>
</html>
```

In the `employees_traversal.html` file, we are importing the `data.js` file, which we examined in the previous section. The `data_json` variable inside the `data.js` file consists of an array of objects that are imported into this HTML page. In the script tags, we are setting up two variables: the `i` variable, which holds a starting counter, and the `employeeCount` variable, which holds the counter of the total number of objects in `data_json`. To retrieve the number of items that exist in an array, we can use the `.length` property that is provided by JavaScript. There are three important supporting blocks for a `for` loop: the condition, the statements, and either the increment or decrement operation based on the condition. Let us take a quick look at these three separately:

```
let i=0;
```

We are initializing the variable `i` to zero and the condition that we are looking for is: if zero is less than the number of items in the constant `data_json`, then proceed into the loop:

```
i<employeeCount
```

If the condition is true, the statements inside the loop are executed, until they hit the incrementing condition:

```
//We are using incremental operation.
i++;
//Incase of decremental operation use i--
```

Once the incrementing operator approaches, the value of the `i` variable is incremented by 1, and it will go back to the initial step of the `for` loop. At the initial step, the condition is again verified to check if `i` is still less than the number of items in `data_json`. If that is true, it will again enter the loop and execute the statements. This process continues to repeat itself until the value of the variable `i` is equal to that of `employeeCount`. At that point, the `for` loop's execution is complete, and the statements inside the `for` loop are maintained as logs in the **Console** window of the browser. Before running the HTML file, `employees_traversal.html`, verify that the `data.json` file is in the same directory as the HTML file. Load this HTML file into a browser of your choice (Chrome, Firefox, or Safari are recommended), and open up the **Console** window by right-clicking on the web page and clicking on **Inspect Element** if you are on Chrome or Safari. The employee numbers should be displayed in the **Console** window:

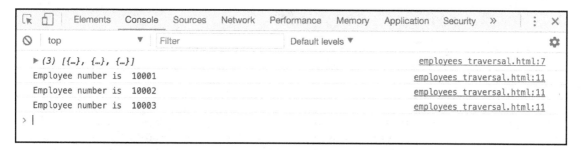

To retrieve the employee's first name and last name, we will concatenate the `first_name` and `last_name` keys in the employee object:

```
//To retrieve the full name
console.log(`Employee's full Name is ${data_json[i].first_name}
${data_json[i].last_name}`);
```

We can use the same technique to retrieve the rest of the keys such as `birth_date`, `gender`, and `hire_date`, with the exception of `designation`. A quick glance at the JSON feed explains that unlike the rest of the keys, a `title` is an object or an array of objects. The `designation` object contains all the titles that the employee has held since joining the company. Some employees have one `title`, while others have more than one; so the former would be an object by itself, while the latter would be an array of objects, each containing a title object. To handle this case, we would have to check if the employee has one title or more than one title. If the person has one `title`, we should print the data, and if the person has more than one title, we have to iterate them through the array of `title` objects to print all the designations that the employee has:

```javascript
for(let i=0;i<employeeCount;i++){
  console.log("Employee number is ", data_json[i].emp_no);
  console.log(`Employee's full Name is ${data_json[i].first_name}
${data_json[i].last_name}`);
  if(data_json[i].designation.title instanceof Array){
    const designationCount = data_json[i].designation.title.length;
    console.log("data_json", data_json[i].designation.title);
    let designations = "";
    for(let j=0;j<designationCount;j++){
      designations+= `, ${data_json[i].designation.title[j]}`;
    }

    console.log(`Employee ${data_json[i].emp_no} has served as
${designations}`)
  }else{
    //Employee with only one designation
    let designation = data_json[i].designation.title;
    console.log(`Employee ${data_json[i].emp_no} has served as
${designation}`)
  }
}
```

The existing code in the script tags has to be replaced with the previous code, provided to retrieve the titles of the employee. In this script, we are using the variables `i` and `employeeCount` from our earlier script. We have introduced a new condition to check if the `title` key inside the `designation` for a particular employee is an Array object. This condition gets the type of the value that the loop is passing in and verifies if it is an instance of an Array object. Let us identify this condition that is checking the instance type:

```javascript
if(data_json[i].designation.title instanceof Array)
```

Once this condition is satisfied, the statements inside the condition are executed. Inside the success condition, we declare three variables. The first variable, j, will hold the counter for the second for loop that iterates through titles.

The second variable is designationCount; it stores the number of items that are available in the titles array. The last variable is designations, which is initialized to an empty string. This variable holds all the titles held by the employee. It stores the list of titles as a string separated by , :

```
for(let j=0;j<designationCount;j++){
    designations+= `, ${data_json[i].designation.title[j]}`;
}
```

In this for loop, the titles of the employee are being built; one title at a time is being added to the designations variable. Once the title has been added to the designations variable, the value of j is incremented and the loop continues until all the title strings are iterated. If the title key is not an array, the execution goes into the else block and the statements in the else block are executed. As there is only one title for that employee, the data is directly printed onto the **Console**.

> Despite the requirement for a for loop, the new ecmascript string modifier can do the trick of concatenating the array into a string that is comma-separated by default. This can be done as:
>
>
>
> ```
> console.log(`${data_json[i].designation.title}`).
> ```
>
> The preceding operation is similar to the code in the else case of the previous employee snippet logic. The `${}` can be used directly for converting our array to a string. The only thing to remember is that, in cases where we need some modifications with respect to concatenation operators other than commas, we may need to use a for loop.

Now that we are familiar with how we can access objects and perform complex operations to extract data, in the next section we will take a look at how JSON data can be modified.

Modifying JSON

JSON retrieved from a JSON feed is always going to be read-only; as such, data feeds do not provide functionality to modify their data from unverified sources. There are many cases where we would want to ingest the data from an external data feed, and then modify that content as per our requirements. An example is a company that is using a data feed that is being supplied by a data vendor, but the data that is being provided is a lot more than the company requires. In such cases, rather than using the whole feed, the company would only extract a part of it, perform certain operations to modify it as per their requirements, and reuse the new JSON object. Let us take our `employee` JSON feed.

Assume that the name of the company was different during different periods. We want to group the employees by company name, which is based on when they joined. Employees who joined the company before 2006 belong to `Company1` and those who joined the company in 2006 or after belong to `Company2`. To represent this change, we add the company key to our JSON feed:

```
<!DOCTYPE html>
<html>
  <head>
    <title>Modify JSON based on joining year</title>
    <script type="text/javascript" src="data.js"></script>
    <script type="text/javascript">
      for(let i in data_json){
        let data = data_json[i];
        //retrieve the year
        const join_year = parseInt(data.hire_date.slice(0,4));

        if(join_year > 2006){
          data.company = "Company1";
        }else{
          data.company = "Company2";
        }

        let message = `Employee ${data.emp_no}
          joined in the year ${join_year}
          belongs to ${data.company}`;

        console.log(message);
      }
    </script>
  </head>
<body>
  <h2>Modifying JSON based on joining year</h2>
  <p>This is a test program to learn how JSON is imported
```

```
      from a feed could be locally modified.</p>
    </p>
  </body>
</html>
```

In the `modify_employee.html` file, we are traversing through the array of employee objects and we are extracting the year in which the employee joined. We are converting this from a string to an integer, so we can use the year value for comparison purposes. We assign the parsed year to the `join_year` variable:

```
let data = data_json[i];
//retrieve the year
const join_year = parseInt(data.hire_date.slice(0,4));
```

In the following code, we are checking to see whether the employee joined the company before 2006; if they joined before 2006, we add the `company` property to the `employee` object and assign the value of `Company1`. If they joined in 2006 or after 2006, we assign the value of `Company2`:

```
if(join_year > 2006){
   data.company = "Company1";
}else{
   data.company = "Company2";
}
```

After a value is assigned to the newly added property company, we build a generic message that will apply to all the employees, irrespective of which company they belong to. We extract the employee number, the year in which the employee joined, and the name of the company to generate that message:

```
let message = `Employee ${data.emp_no}
 joined in the year ${join_year}
 belongs to ${data.company}`;
console.log(message);
```

When `modify_employee.html` is run from the web browser, the script to perform the modifications is run and the output is logged to the **Console**:

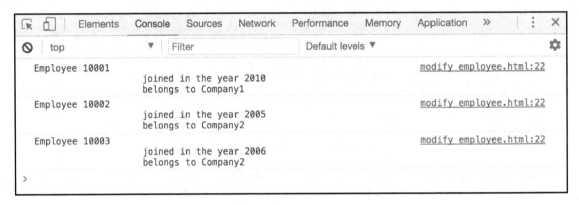

Summary

This chapter addressed the core concepts of how to handle static JSON feeds. We began by importing an external JSON object into our HTML file, and looped through the complex array of objects to parse and extract the required data. We used the while and `for` loops to loop through the array and used conditions to target our search. We completed this chapter by locally modifying the existing JSON feed and adding a new property, the employee object. Now that we have mastered accessing JSON from a static file, it is time for us to make some asynchronous calls to fetch some active JSON over HTTP.

AJAX Requests with JSON 3

JSON is considered today to be the most popular data interchange format. In the previous chapter, we saw an example that used a JSON feed as a data store. In this chapter, let's make the data a little more dynamic. The following list provides a glimpse of all the topics that will be covered in this chapter:

- Step-based procedure for how a web application operates
- Learning synchronous versus asynchronous requests
- Setting up the requirements for making an AJAX request
- Hosting JSON
  - Handling AJAX responses using callbacks, promises, and generators
- Parsing the JSON response

HTML, client-side JavaScript, and CSS provide the structural, behavioral, and presentational aspects, respectively. Dynamic web development is all about data transfer between two parties, the client and the server. We use programs such as a web server, a database, and a server-side programming language to fetch and store dynamic data. Let's take a look at the process behind the scenes that facilitates successful operations on the data.

Basic web operations

When a user opens up a web browser and types any URL – for example, `http://www.packtpub.com/` – the following sequence of activities takes place :

1. The browser makes a request to the **Internet Service Provider** (**ISP**) to perform a reverse lookup of the IP address by providing the domain name.

2. Once the IP address is retrieved, the request is then forwarded to the machine that owns the IP address. At that point, there is a web server that is waiting to consume the request; the web server could be one of the top web servers, such as Apache, IIS, Tomcat, and Nginx.

3. The web server receives the request and looks at the headers that are part of the HTTP request; those headers pass the information about the request that was made to the web server.

4. Once the web server parses those headers, it routes the request over to a server-side programming application that is responsible for handling this request. The application could be written in PHP, C#/ASP.NET, Java/JSP, and so on.

5. This responsible server-side language takes the request, understands it, and performs the necessary business logic to complete the request. A few examples of such HTTP requests are loading a web page and clicking the **Contact us** link on a website. There can be complex HTTP requests too, where the data has to be validated, cleansed, and/or retrieved from a data storage application such as a database, a file server, or a caching server.

Synchronous vs. asynchronous

HTTP requests can be made in two ways; synchronously and asynchronously.

A **synchronous request** is a blocking request, where everything has to be done in an orderly fashion, one step after another, and where the following step has to wait until the previous one has completed its execution. Let's assume that there are four independent components on a web page when the page is loaded; if one component takes a long time during execution, the rest of the page is going to wait for it until its execution is complete. If execution fails, the page load fails too. One other example is when there is a poll and a rating component on the web page; if the user chooses to answer the poll and give a rating to fulfill these requests, two requests have to be sent out one after the other if we go with a synchronous requesting mechanism.

Polling

In the previous poll terminology, do not get confused by the HTTP long polling technique. It's altogether a different mechanism. Follow this link for more information: `https://en.wikipedia.org/wiki/Push_technology#Long_polling`.

To tackle the issue of synchronous requests, the development community has gradually made progress in the field of **asynchronous HTTP requests**. The first product to come out that allowed asynchronous requests was IFrame tags, introduced by Microsoft; they used IFrames via Internet Explorer to load content asynchronously. After IFrame, next in line to revolutionize the Internet was the XML HTTP ActiveX control. In later years, all the browsers adopted this control under the new XMLHttpRequest JavaScript object, which is part of the XMLHttpRequest API. The XMLHttpRequest API is used to make an HTTP (or HTTPS) call to a web server. It can be used to make both synchronous and asynchronous calls. Asynchronous requests allow developers to divide web pages into multiple components independent of each other, thereby saving a lot of memory by sending data on demand.

Jesse James Garrett named this phenomenon "AJAX". In **AJAX** (**Asynchronous JavaScript and XML**), web requests are made via JavaScript and the data interchange originally happened in XML. The "X" in AJAX was originally considered to be XML, but today it can be any data interchange format, such as XML, JSON, text file, or even HTML. The data format being used for the data transfer has to be mentioned in the MIME type headers. In Chapter 1, *Getting Started with JSON*, we have already highlighted why JSON is the preferred data interchange format. Let us take a quick look at what we would need to make our first AJAX call with JSON data.

Essentially, web developers can use the principles of AJAX to fetch data on demand to make websites more responsive and interactive; it is very important to understand what generates that demand. The trigger for such a demand for data is commonly an event that occurs on the web page. An **event** can be described as a reaction to an action that was performed; for example, ringing a bell produces a vibration inside the bell that generates the sound. Here, ringing a bell is the event, while the sound that is produced is the reaction to the event. There can be multiple events on a web page; a few such events are clicking a button, submitting a form, hovering over a link, and choosing an option from a drop-down, all of which are very common events. We have to come up with a way in which they are programmatically handled when these events occur.

Requirements for AJAX

AJAX is an asynchronous two-way communication between the browser that is considered to be the client and a live web server via HTTP (or HTTPS). We can run a live server locally, using tools such as Apache, IIS, or node.js. We are choosing node.js to be our main server-side platform.

Setting up a node.js server

Perform the following steps to build a node.js server:

1. Download the setup from the following link: `https://nodejs.org/en/`. The reader needs to select the **LTS (long-term support)** executable so that we receive node.js community support for a long period of time.

2. The installation is a simple one-click setup procedure, you just need to follow the steps. If you are planning to install via terminal, here is the link for the required steps: `https://nodejs.org/en/download/package-manager/`.

3. Once the installation is complete, we are all set to write our first server-side program to generate and host a live JSON feed. Run the following commands in the terminal to create a file in the directory:

```
$ mkdir test-node-app
$ cd test-node-app
$ npm init
```

The `npm init` command comes with a questionnaire that needs to be completed before setting up the app. This command is important so as to create `package.json`, which acts as a register for all the modules and packages installed. It also plays a major role in managing your application. For more details, follow this link: `https://docs.npmjs.com/cli/init`.

4. Create an app file named `app.js`. This file contains the code that builds a server. This can be referred from the following code:

```javascript
const http = require('http');
const port = 3300;
http.createServer((req, res) => {
    res.writeHead(200, {
      "Content-Type": "text/plain"
    });
    res.write("Hello Readers!");
    res.end();
}).listen(port);
console.log(`Node Server is running on port : ${port}`)
```

Let us get the working output first, followed by an explanation of the preceding code.

5. Once the snippet is ready to go, run the command as follows:

```
node app.js
```

If everything is perfectly coded, we get the following output:

```
Node Server is running on port : 3300
```

To perform the server request activity, we should open up a browser in the operating system and access `http://localhost:3300`; we should then get the following output in our browser document body.

```
Hello Readers!
```

Once we receive this message we are assured that our web server is up and running.

Let us go over, step by step, how things work in the preceding script:

1. The first line includes the HTTP native module already present in the node API. This module provides all the functionality required to build an HTTP server.
2. The instance of HTTP consists of several methods for the variety of functionalities it provides. To fulfil our aim, we are using a `createServer` method, which, when invoked, creates a server and returns an `HTTP` server instance.
3. You can pass a callback function in the `createServer` method as a parameter so that whenever a server receives an HTTP request it gets called and sends the desired response to the client. Though the callback is optional to pass as a parameter, it is important for us to perform various operations on the received request and return the response accordingly.
4. Finally, the most important and mandatory step is to listen on a stipulated port. This can be achieved by invoking the listen method provided by the HTTP server instance.
5. Woot! Our HTTP server is ready, but it responds to the client in a different string data format from "Hello Readers!", and that needs to be changed to JSON.

Web applications can be built in any language, and JSON can be used as the data interchange language between web applications powered by any server-side stack. Let's take this knowledge of server-side programming and move forward on our journey so that we can implement this in powerful web applications.

Hosting JSON

In this section, we will be creating a node script that will allow us to send a JSON feedback to the user upon a successful request. Let's take a look at the app.js file that accomplishes this task:

```
const http = require('http');
const port = 3300;
http.createServer((req, res) => {
    res.writeHead(200, {
        "Content-Type": "application/json"
    });
    res.write(JSON.stringify({
        greet : "Hello Readers!"
    }));
    res.end();
}).listen(port);
console.log(`Node Server is running on port : ${port}`)
```

The changes required to send JSON data are highlighted in the preceding snippet. The above script consists of a JSON object with greet as the key and Hello Readers! as the value. The object is first stringified as the responses provided are always in string or buffer form. Moreover, we need to provide the content-type as application/json. The Content-Type gets set inside the header of response so that the browser may identify the response type as mentioned.

Let's increase the complexity of JSON by using the example of student data. Create the JSON file student_data.json as follows:

```
//student_data.json
[{
    "studentid": 101,
    "firstname": "John",
    "lastname": "Doe",
    "classes": ["Business Research", "Economics", "Finance"]
},
{
    "studentid": 102,
    "firstname": "Jane",
    "lastname": "Dane",
    "classes": ["Marketing", "Economics", "Finance"]
}]
```

Include the `student_data.json` file in our server script file as follows:

```
const http = require('http');
const port = 3300;
const studentsData = require('./student_data.json');
http.createServer((req, res) => {
    res.writeHead(200, {
        "Content-Type": "application/json"
    });
    res.write(JSON.stringify(studentsData));
    res.end();
}).listen(port);
console.log(`Node Server is running on port : ${port}`)
```

In this node script, we have created a basic `studentsData` array and are generating the JSON feed for that array. The students array contains basic student information such as the first name, last name, student ID, and the classes that the student has enrolled in.

Next, we need to access this file via the node web server and navigate to `http://localhost:3300` to get the following output:

As shown in the preceding screenshot, when the file is run using the node web server, the server takes the request, processes it, and outputs the JSON feed that delivers the student data.

Making your first AJAX call

Now that we have an active JSON data feed, it is about time to make our first AJAX call. We will look at different approaches to making an AJAX call; this technology and the way it is used have evolved over a period of time with the aim of improving performance. The first approach will use basic JavaScript so that we understand what happens behind the scenes when an AJAX call is made. Once we understand the concept of AJAX, we will use some popular libraries to make the same AJAX call but with some variations. Let's take a look at our first approach, using basic JavaScript by creating a `basic.html` file with the following template:

```html
<!DOCTYPE html>
<html>
<head>
  <title>First AJAX script</title>
  <script type="text/javascript" src="basic.js"></script>
</head>
<body>
  <h2>Include external Javascript to make an ajax call</h2>
  <p>This is a test program to make our first AJAX call using
javascript</p>
</body>
</html>
```

We will begin with our basic `basic.html` file that loads an external JavaScript file. This JavaScript file performs the AJAX call to fetch the `students` JSON feed.

Let's take a look at `basic.js`:

```javascript
const request = new XMLHttpRequest();
request.open('GET', 'http://localhost:3300');
request.onreadystatechange = function(){
    if((request.status==200) && (request.readyState==4)){
        console.log(request.responseText);
    }
}
request.send();
```

This is the original way in which an AJAX call is made to a live web server; let's break this script into pieces and investigate it piece by piece:

```javascript
const request = new XMLHttpRequest();
```

In the preceding snippet, we are creating an instance of the XMLHttpRequest object. The XMLHttpRequest object lets us make asynchronous calls to the server, thus allowing us to treat sections in the page as separate components. It comes with powerful properties such as readystate, response, and responseText, and methods such as open, onuploadprogress, onreadystatechange, and send. Let's look at how we can use the request object that we have created to open an AJAX request:

```
request.open('GET', 'http://localhost:3300');
```

XMLHttpRequest, by default, opens up an asynchronous request; here we will specify the method in which the live feed has to be contacted. As we will not be passing any data, we choose the HTTP GET method to send the data over to our live web server. While working on an asynchronous request, we should never have a blocking script; we can deal with this by setting up callbacks. A **callback** is a set of scripts that wait for a response and will be fired on receiving that response. This behavior facilitates non-blocking code.

We are setting up a callback and are assigning the callback to a method called onreadystatechange, as shown in the following snippet:

```
request.onreadystatechange = function(){
    if((request.status==200) && (request.readyState==4)){
        console.log(request.responseText);
    }
}
```

The placeholder method, onreadystatechange, looks for a property in the request object called readyState; whenever the value of readyState changes, the onreadystatechange event is fired. The readyState property keeps track of the progress of the XMLHttpRequest that is made. In the preceding screenshot, we can see the callback has a conditional statement that is verifying that the value of readyState is 4, meaning that the server has received the XMLHttpRequest that was made by the client and a response is ready. Let's take a quick look at the available values for readyState:

readyState	Description
0	The request hasn't been initialized
1	Server connection established
2	The server has received the request
3	The server is processing the request
4	The request has been processed and the response is ready

In the earlier snippet, we are also looking for another property called the status; this is the HTTP status code that is coming back from the server. Status code 200 represents a successful transaction, while status code 400 is a bad request and 404 means **Page Not Found**. Other common status codes are 401, which means the user has requested a page that is available only for authorized users, and 500, which is an **Internal Server Error**.

We have created the XMLHttpRequest object and opened the connection; we have also added a callback to perform an event when the request is successful. One thing to keep in mind is that the request hasn't yet been made; we are only laying the foundational work for the request. We will use the send() method to send the request over to the server, as shown:

```
request.send();
```

In our onreadystateChange callback, we are logging the response that is sent by the web server to the console window.

Now, when we run our code for the first time, the following error can be seen in the **Console** tab of the browser:

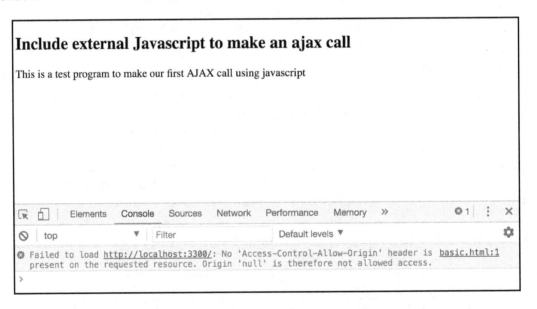

The cause of the error is when the loaded document has a different domain name in the browser's URL locator and the AJAX requests a different URL. This is again due to the browser's policy of **cross-origin resource sharing** (**CORS**). The following link provides details about CORS: https://developer.mozilla.org/en-US/docs/Web/HTTP/CORS.

To fix our issue we need to handle it at server side, providing CORS support. To do this, we need to add `Access-Control-Allow-Origin` in our `writeHead` method or the response object `res`. The value should be `*`, which means the access is granted to any domain or request. This is shown as follows:

```
res.writeHead(200, {
    "Content-Type": "application/json",
    "Access-Control-Allow-Origin": "*",
});
```

Make sure that this is setting is not the same in the production environment. In production, we need to specify the domain name example :

```
"Access-Control-Allow-Origin":"www.differentdomain.com"
```

Getting back to our code, let's take a quick look at what the response looks like:

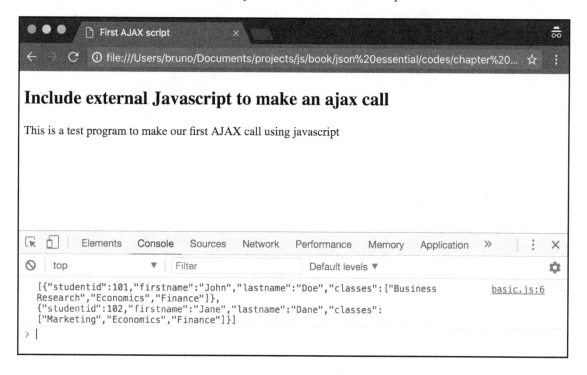

One way to confirm that this is an AJAX request is by looking at the first request in the **Network** tab of the browser, near the **Console** tab, where an asynchronous call is made to the `localhost:3300` address and the response comes back with an HTTP status code of `200 OK`. Since the HTTP `status` value is `200`, the execution of the callback will be successful and it will output the `students` JSON feed.

With the advent of powerful JavaScript libraries such as jQuery, Scriptaculous, Dojo, and ExtJS, we have moved away from the archaic process of making an AJAX request. One thing to keep in mind is that though we do not use this process, libraries will still be using this process under the hood; so having an idea of how the `XMLHttpRequest` object works is very important. jQuery is a very popular JavaScript library; it has a growing community with a lot of developers. As the jQuery library is distributed under the MIT License, users are able to utilize this library free of cost.

jQuery is a very simple, powerful library with fantastic documentation and a strong user community that makes a developer's life very easy. Let's take a quick detour and write our customary Hello World program in jQuery:

```
<!DOCTYPE html>
<html>
  <head>
      <title>Hello world using jQuery</title>
      <!-- Go to https://code.jquery.com/ for more details -->
      <script src="https://code.jquery.com/jquery-3.2.1.min.js"
integrity="sha256-hwg4gsxgFZhOsEEamdOYGBf13FyQuiTwlAQgxVSNgt4="
crossorigin="anonymous"></script>
      <script>
      $(document).ready(() => {
          console.log("Hello world!");
      })
      </script>
  </head>
  <body>
      <h2>Hello world using jquery</h2>
      <p>This is a Hello world program using jquery</p>
  </body>
</html>
```

In the preceding screenshot, we are importing the jQuery library into our HTML file, and in the second set of script tags, we are using the special character $, or jQuery. Similar to the concept of the namespace in object-oriented programming, the jQuery functionality is namespaced to the special character $ by default. jQuery has been a champion of unobtrusive JavaScript. After $, we call the document object and check whether it has loaded onto the page; then, we assign a callback function that will be triggered by the completion of a document load event. document here is the document object that holds the HTML element structure. The output of this program is going be the Hello World! string that will be outputted to our console window.

In an upcoming section, we are going to study the traditional ways of handling a JSON on serving a client request. We may already have some brief knowledge of callbacks, which is one of the asynchronous way of handling a server request. Let us start with callbacks in some more details and also study some more evolved methods too.

Traditional callbacks

The callback is a simple, anonymous function that is passed as a parameter and invoked when required inside another function's scope. Consider the following snippet:

```
function greetAll(callback){
 console.log("Hello Readers!");
 console.log(`Greeting from the ${callback()}`)
}
greetAll(()=>{
 return "Author";
})
```

In the preceding code, we have a greetAll function that contains a simple parameter named callback. On invocation of the greetAll function, we have passed an anonymous function as a parameter. Henceforth, greetAll is executed in a programming context that performs the following stepwise operation:

1. Firstly, it logs **Hello Readers!**
2. While the second log is being executed from left to right, it invokes the parameter named callback sequentially to the operation, thus printing **Greeting from the Author**

Note that the callback can be called once all the operations of the greetAll function are completed, or it can also be called before other operations, depending on the functionality required. Such a mechanism can be used to handle an asynchronous event. Consider the request we made at the address `localhost:3300`; it was an asynchronous request made using an AJAX method in the browser. Let's relate this study and apply a callback to AJAX calls using a jQuery AJAX GET method:

```
<!--jquery-ajax.html-->
<!DOCTYPE html>
<html>
<head>
    <title>Ajax using jquery</title>
    <!-- Go to https://code.jquery.com/ for more details -->
    <script src="https://code.jquery.com/jquery-3.2.1.min.js"
integrity="sha256-hwg4gsxgFZhOsEEamdOYGBf13FyQuiTwlAQgxVSNgt4="
crossorigin="anonymous"></script>
    <script>
    $(document).ready(() => {
        $('#getFeed').click(()=>{
            $.getJSON('http://localhost:3300/',(jsonData)=>{
                console.log("jsonData", jsonData);
            })
        })
    })
    </script>
</head>
<body>
    <h2>AJAX using jquery</h2>
    <input type="button" id="getFeed" value="Get Feed" />
</body>
</html>
```

In the preceding `script` tag, we have requested that our node server get student data. In this example, we have passed a callback as a second parameter to the invocation of the `$.getJSON` method of jQuery. This callback handles the data received upon request completion. Similarly, if you looked carefully, you will have seen that there is one more callback mechanism used in the preceding snippet. Yes, your guess is right! It's jQuery's click method, which accepts a callback that provides a mechanism to write code on click event occurrences in the browser.

By now, you have got the whole idea of callbacks and why they are used. Next, let's study some advanced asynchronous data handling mechanisms.

Handling asynchronousity using a promise

Though traditionally a callback is the most widely used and often the best way to serve async behavior, it still fails to adhere to some standard requirements for code patterns. A few of the shortcomings faced are as follows:

- If you return any data in callbacks passed to some API library, such as jQuery in the above case, you will never know how the return data in that callback is handled in the code of that library. Consider the code illustrated below :

```
$.getJSON('http://localhost:3300/',(jsonData)=>{
    console.log("jsonData", jsonData);
    return jsonData;
})
```

The `return` statement `return jsonData;` in the previous case makes no sense as to where it goes.

- Another major issue is handling an error exception. Consider the following code:

```
$.getJSON('http://localhost:3300/',(jsonData)=>{
    console.log("jsonData", jsonData);
    throws "someError 500";
})
```

If any errors happen accidentally or are explicitly thrown, as shown in the preceding snippet, there is no way to handle that error at callback level. We do definitely have the infamous `try{}catch(e){}` block to handle it, but that's not recommended for use every time you write some code in the callback.

- The next issue is not that major but still considerable: code readability. Using too many callbacks sequentially creates a *bullhead* structure known as callback hell. To learn more about it, follow this link: `http://callbackhell.com/`.

To mitigate such issues the concept of *promises* was invented. Let us implement a promise for our code. While doing so we need to replace the previous traditional callback with a `'thenable'` chain as follows:

```
$.getJSON('http://localhost:3300/')
.then((jsonData)=>{
    console.log("jsonData", jsonData);
    return jsonData;
})
.then((jsonDataAgain)=>{
    console.log("recieved jsonData again", jsonDataAgain);
```

```
        return jsonDataAgain;
    })
```

There are two simple principles behind promises, based on which way the promise tower works:

- **Resolved**: Being resolved is a state of promise in which the functionality is successfully completed as intended. In the previous case, we requested `localhost:3300` and we received a successful response as `jsonData` with `status-code 200` in response headers. The successful response is received in the callback of the `then` method.
- **Rejected**: Being rejected is the state of promise in which the functionality fails to complete as intended. To demonstrate this, let's throw an error in the callback of `then`:

```
$.getJSON('http://localhost:3300/')
.then((jsonData)=>{
    throw "Error : Something is wrong";
    return jsonData;
})
.then((jsonDataAgain)=>{
    console.log("recieved jsonData again", jsonDataAgain);
    return jsonDataAgain;
})
.catch((error)=>{
    console.log("Error handled", error);
})
```

The explicitly thrown error in the preceding case can be handled using a `catch` method of the promise. All the errors that can happen while sending a request or after a request has been received can be caught in the `catch` method.

Note that whatever is returned in the callback of the first `then` method can be received by the adjacent `then` method of the same level. Hence, in the preceding case, the same data can be received.

New ECMAScript generators

If you hate the callback style in JavaScript or prefer blocking or pausing an asynchronous execution and resuming it when data is received, you will love what the new ECMAScript has introduced in JavaScript: generators.

To put it simply, generators are iterable functions that:

- Generate some kind of data
- Use the `yield` keyword to pause the pause or resume the execution
- Syntactically denoted by `function *functionName` or `function* functionName`
- Use continuous infinite loops if we need to continuously yield on some event we are listening for

These are the specifications of a generator. To clarify the definition, let's implement the concept in our AJAX example.

The asynchronous line in our code is `$.getJSON('http://localhost:3300/')`. Let's segregate it in a generator function. To write a generator function we need to follow the guidelines shown as follows:

1. Include the generator syntax:

```
function* generateData(){}
```

2. Include a `yield` statement:

```
function* generateData(){
    yield $.getJSON('http://localhost:3300/');
}
```

3. Once the generator function is ready, we can call it normally just like a function invocation:

```
const generatorInst = generateData();
```

The `generateData` function returns an iterator object and not the response data.

4. To get the response data, we need to call the `next` method if there is an iterator object. Here, in the following example, we call the `next` method on the click of a button:

```
$('#getFeed').click(()=>{
    console.log(generatorInst.next());
})
```

We will get the following output on the first click:

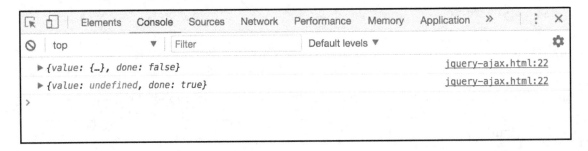

5. Once we get the data and click on the same button for a second time, we receive the following output:

You may have noticed that value of the `done` key is `true` and the `value` key is `undefined`. This means that the execution has reached the end of the generator function. No more iterations are going to occur or are left to get the data. So from the second click onward, we receive this similar kind of data.

To generate the data on all the clicks, we need to yield the data to infinity. This can be done with the following changes to the generator function `generateData`:

```
function* generateData(){
    while(true){
        yield $.getJSON('http://localhost:3300/');
    }
}
```

Now, every time you click on the **get feed** button you will observe that we can fetch the response data.

To recap everything, by now you have made AJAX requests using callbacks, promises, and generators. Each mechanism has its own advantages and practiced with respect to trending ecmascript versions. Once we learn the JSON fetching mechanisms in the browser, we are moving towards parsing the received data and utilizing it for other required operations.

Parsing JSON data

Now that we are familiar with jQuery, let us trigger an AJAX request on an event such as a button click:

```html
<!--jquery-ajax.html-->
<!DOCTYPE html>
<html>
<head>
    <title>Ajax using jquery</title>
    <!-- Go to https://code.jquery.com/ for more details -->
    <script src="https://code.jquery.com/jquery-3.2.1.min.js"
integrity="sha256-hwg4gsxgFZhOsEEamdOYGBf13FyQuiTwlAQgxVSNgt4="
crossorigin="anonymous"></script>
    <script>
$(document).ready(() => {
    $('#getFeed').click(()=>{
        $.getJSON('http://localhost:3300/',(jsonData)=>{
            if(jsonData){
                $.each(jsonData, (key, value)=>{
                    $('#feedContainerList')
                    .append(`<li>Student Id is ${value.studentid}
                        and the student name is ${value.firstname}
                        and ${value.lastname}
                        </li>`);
                })
            }
```

```
                })
            })
        })
    })
    </script>
</head>
<body>
    <h2>AJAX using jquery</h2>
    <input type="button" id="getFeed" value="Get Feed" />
    <div id="feedContainer">
        <div id="feedContainerList">

        </div>
    </div>
</body>
</html>
```

In this snippet, let us begin by observing the HTML document object. We have a div element that has an empty unordered list. The aim of this script is to populate the unordered list with list items on the click of a button. The input button element has an id with the value "getFeed", and the click event handler will be tied to this button. Since AJAX is asynchronous and as we are assigning a callback to this button, no AJAX calls are made to our live server when the document object is loaded. The HTML structure alone is loaded onto the page, and the events are tied to these elements.

When the button is clicked on, we are using the method getJSON to make an AJAX call to the live web server to retrieve the JSON data. Since we are getting an array of students, we pass the retrieved data into jQuery's each iterator to retrieve one element at a time. Inside the iterator, we are building a string, which is appended as a list item to the "feedContainerList" unordered list element:

On loading the document, as we are only binding our events to the HTML elements, there will not be any behavioral changes unless we click on the button. Once we click on the button, the unordered list will be populated.

Summary

Since the rise in popularity of the XMLHttpRequest object, it has become a boon for web developers. In this chapter, we began with the basics, such as what we need to make an AJAX request. Furthermore, we moved ahead and understood the basic concept of how an XMLHttpRequest object is responsible for making an asynchronous request. Then we took a leap into one of the most powerful JavaScript Libraries, jQuery, to perform AJAX operations using jQuery. This is just the beginning of our journey into AJAX; in the next chapter, we will be looking at more complex cases where AJAX is used, the cases where cross-domain asynchronous requests fail, and how JSON saves the day by allowing us to make cross-domain asynchronous calls.

Cross-Domain Asynchronous Requests

4

In `Chapter 3`, *AJAX Requests with JSON*, we used jQuery's `getJSON` method to ingest the students' JSON feed; in this chapter, we will take a step forward and send request parameters over to the server. We have already come across cross-domain requests in the third chapter; we will be exploring cross-domain requests in more depth in this chapter. Here is the content of the chapter:

- Making GET and POST AJAX calls with JSON data
- The problem with cross-domain AJAX calls
- Introduction to JSONP
- Implementing JSONP

Let's start by understanding the concept of APIs.

The API story

Data feeds are often large amounts of data that are made available; the data that is part of such feeds is normally generic and can be considered too heavy for a targeted search. For example, in the students JSON feed, we are exposing the whole list of student information that is available. For a data vendor who is looking for students who are enrolled in certain courses or who reside in a given ZIP code to hire them as interns, this feed is going to be generic. It is common to see development teams build Application Programming Interfaces (APIs), to give such data vendors numerous ways to target their search. This is a win-win situation for both the data vendor and for the company that owns the information, since the data vendor only gets the information that they are looking for and the data supplier only sends the requested data, thereby saving a lot of bandwidth and server resources.

Making GET and POST AJAX calls with JSON data

It is important to understand that both synchronous and asynchronous calls are made over HTTP, so the data transfer process is the same. The most popular methods of transferring data from the client machine to the server machine are GET and POST. The most common request method in HTTP is GET. When a client requests a web page, the web server uses the URL to process the HTTP request. Any other parameters that are appended to the URL serve as the data that is being sent from the client to the server. Since the parameters are part of the URL, it is important to make a clear distinction between when and when not to use the GET request method. The GET method should be used to pass idempotent information such as a page number, a link address, or the limits and offsets that are a part of pagination. Keep in mind that there is a size constraint as to how much data can be transferred via the GET request method.

We will be working with a modified students API where we will be able to query complete student information—the ZIP code they live in, the classes that they take, and so on—and use a combination search to find students who live in a certain area and are taking a certain class.

To see the code for this chapter, see the following GitHub link: `https://github.com/bron10/json-essentials-book/tree/master/chapter%204`.

Now let's look at the URL for our first targeted search—by ZIP code:

```
http://localhost:3300/?zipcode=400002
```

This API call will return all the students that reside in the given ZIP code area. So in our case, we have following output:

```
[{"studentid":102,"firstname":"Jane","lastname":"Dane","zipcode":400002,"classes":
["Marketing","Economics","Finance"]}]
```

In the preceding example, we received the details of a single student who has the ZIP code 400002. To achieve this output we need to make some modifications in our Node server app.js file as follows. The modifications in the following code are highlighted:

```javascript
const http = require('http');
const port = 3300;
const urlObject = require('url');
const querystring = require('querystring');
let studentsData = require('./student_data.json');
http.createServer((req, res) => {
    let url = req.url;
    const urlParsedObject = urlObject.parse(req.url);
    const pathname = urlParsedObject.pathname;
    const queryObject = querystring.parse(urlParsedObject.query);
    res.writeHead(200, {
      "Content-Type": "application/json",
      "Access-Control-Allow-Origin" : "*"
    });
switch(pathname){
case '/':
    let student = studentsData.filter((student)=>{
      return student.zipcode == queryObject.zipcode;
    })
    res.write(JSON.stringify(student));
    res.end();
    break;
}
}).listen(port);
console.log(`Node Server is running on port : ${port}`)
```

Some brief info regarding the preceding code; firstly, we have added two native node modules, require('url') and require('queryString'). The former provides methods to parse the data from the whole URL string. In our case, we have a request URL. This is used for simply parsing the query of an URL. Hence, here we convert ?zipcode=400002 to a JSON object {zipcode : 400002} so that it can be accessed easily.

For more information on the queryString package, see:
`https://nodejs.org/docs/latest-v7.x/api/querystring.html`.

Also, for URL package information, see: `https://nodejs.org/docs/latest-v7.x/api/url.html`.

Once we get the query data we loop over the studentsData array and filter out all the student data using the zipcode key. The resultant data is written in response and, after the call of the end method of the response, the data is sent to the client.

One more thing to notice is the switch case. This is used to differentiate all the routes so that more routes can be added just by inserting one more case in the switch with ease. To recap about routes, they are the requested URL that server accepts the validity of and adheres to by providing a response.

The following is the code snippet for get-students.html:

```
<!DOCTYPE html>
<html>
<head>
    <title>Get all students</title>
    <!-- Go to https://code.jquery.com/ for more details -->
    <script
src="https://code.jquery.com/jquery-3.2.1.min.js"
integrity="sha256-hwg4gsxgFZhOsEEamdOYGBf13FyQuiTwlAQgxVSNgt4="
crossorigin="anonymous"></script>
    <script>
    $(document).ready(() => {
        $.ajax({
            "url" : "http://localhost:3300",
            "type" : "GET",
            "data" : {},
            "dataTYPE":"JSON"
        })
        .done((data)=>{
            console.log(data);
        })
    })
    </script>
</head>
<body>
    <h2>Get all students</h2>
    <p>Retrieve the students information of all students</p>
</body>
</html>
```

In this call we start by importing the jQuery library; we can start using the $ variable as we have jQuery on the page. We begin by adding a callback that is fired when the document is ready. We are using the AJAX method for this example as it allows us to make GET and POST requests.

It is not necessary to explicitly mention when the type is GET, but it helps us build consistency with our code.

In our AJAX call we begin by setting the URL property of the link to our API call to retrieve student information; we specify that this will be performed via the HTTP GET method. The fourth property that we are setting is the dataType property; this is used to mention the type of the data that we are expecting to be returned. As we are working with the students feed, we will have to set the dataType property to JSON. It is important to note the done callback fired when the server sends a response back to our asynchronous request. We are passing the data that is sent over from the server as a response, initiating the callback.

 .done is a successful callback validation similar to readyState=4 and request.status=200; we looked at this in Chapter 3, *AJAX Requests with JSON Data*, while making asynchronous calls using JavaScript.

The following is the output:

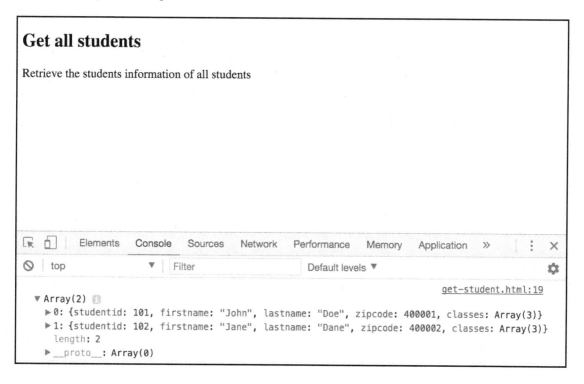

In the **Console** window, we can view the JSON feed response that comes back from the server. This JSON feed contains a lot of information, as it gets the data for all the students. Now let us fetch the student records based on the ZIP code. For this example, we will be using the zipcode parameter and will asynchronously pass a value to the server via the HTTP GET method. This API call will serve this purpose for data vendors who want to search for interns who are available in a specific area:

```
$.ajax({
"url" : "http://localhost:3300",
 "type" : "GET",
 "data" : {"zipcode" : "400001"},
 "dataTYPE":"JSON"
})
.done((data)=>{
 console.log(data);
})
```

In the previous example, we start by importing the jQuery library and we bind a callback to ready the event that is fired when the document has loaded. It is important to notice that we are sending a key-value pair for the ZIP code using the data property:

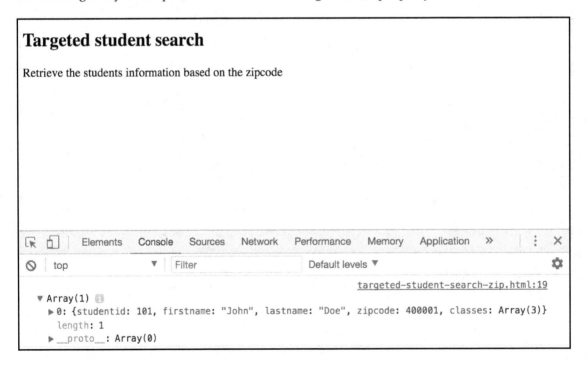

Once the call is fired, we log the response to the **Console** window. The ZIP code 400001 matches one user, and the student information is passed back via the JSON feed. Targeted searches help us narrow down our results, thereby providing us with the data that we are looking for; the next target search will be to retrieve data using a certain class that a student is enrolled in.

Let's switch the search criteria from the ZIP code to the class that a student has enrolled into:

```
http://localhost:3300/?class=Economics
```

In this example, the URL will return information for all the students that have enrolled for the class Economics. Server-side, the following changes are needed in the URL with the path case '/':

```
case '/':
  let student = studentsData.filter((student)=>{
    if(queryObject.zipcode){
      return (student.zipcode == queryObject.zipcode);
    }
    else if(~((student.classes).indexOf(queryObject.class))){
      return student;
    }
  })
  if(student.length==0){
    student = studentsData;
  }
  res.write(JSON.stringify(student));
  res.end();
break;
```

Moving to our client-side, we need to run the following HTML code in the browser:

```
<!DOCTYPE html>
<html>
<head>
    <title>Targeted student search</title>
    <!-- Go to https://code.jquery.com/ for more details -->
    <script
  src="https://code.jquery.com/jquery-3.2.1.min.js"
  integrity="sha256-hwg4gsxgFZhOsEEamdOYGBf13FyQuiTwlAQgxVSNgt4="
  crossorigin="anonymous"></script>
    <script>
    $(document).ready(() => {
        $.ajax({
            "url" : "http://localhost:3300",
            "type" : "GET",
```

```
            "data" : {"class" : "Economics"},
            "dataTYPE":"JSON"
        })
        .done((data)=>{
          console.log(data);
        })
    })
    </script>
</head>
<body>
    <h2>Targeted student search</h2>
    <p>Retrieve the students information based on classes thy are enrolled
in.</p>
</body>
</html>
```

The previous example is the same as the targeted search with ZIP code; here we are replacing the ZIP code information with the class information. We are retrieving all the students who have enrolled for Economics:

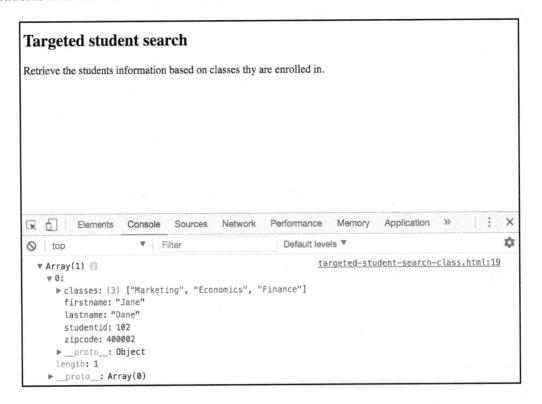

We have seen multiple examples of making asynchronous calls via the HTTP GET method; now it is time for us to push the data onto the server in order to add a student using our API. The last call in our API is powered by the HTTP POST method for adding a student.

The POST request method is commonly used while sending data that is large and non-trivial. Unlike the GET method, the data is transferred through the HTTP message body; we can use tools such as Fiddler and the developer tools available in the browser to track the data that is going out through the HTTP message body. The data that is being passed through the POST method cannot be bookmarked or cached, unlike the GET method. The POST method is often used to send data while using forms.

To handle a POST request on the server side we need to make the following changes at the node server. We are going to add one more case in our switch conditions, for /addUser:

```
case '/addUser':
    let jsonString = '';
    req.on('data', (chunk) => {
        jsonString += chunk;
    });
    req.on('end', () => {
        let parseJSON = JSON.parse(jsonString);
        studentsData.push(jsonString);
        res.end(JSON.stringify(jsonString));
    });
break;
```

To provide brief information about handling data on the server side :

- By default we don't receive the body information in the request parameter directly. Instead, we need to listen on the request object data listener for the requested data. This factual antidote means that we will be collecting the request data on the event data listener. Once all the data is completely collected from request, it will automatically fire the request end event.
- The callback of the event end listener does the simple operation of pushing the data in the student array and responding by sending the whole student data back to the client. Make sure that you change the identifier keyword of the studentsData from const to show which is being used while importing.

So, returning to the client, the URL needed for our post request is as follows:

```
http://localhost:3300/addUser
```

As this is an HTTP POST method, none of the data that is being passed in is visible. Let's move forward with our scripts to access these calls; the first script will be to access the API call that provides information for all the students.

We will be using our addUser call to add a student on the fly. This helps the development teams add student information into our database from external resources. For example, say we are a student information aggregator and we sell consolidated student information to multiple data vendors. For us to aggregate all this information, we might be aggregating it via spiders, where a script would go to a website and fetch the data, or external resources, where the data will be unstructured. So we will structure our data and use this addUser API call to ingest the structured student data information into our data storage. Simultaneously, we can expose this method to trusted data vendors who would like to store the student information that is not available with us, thereby helping them to make our data storage a single point data location. It is a win-win for both the companies as we get more student information and our data vendors get to store their student information on a remote location. Now let's take a look at how this addUser post call will be made:

```html
//add-user.html
<!DOCTYPE html>
<html>
<head>
    <title>Adding a student</title>
    <!-- Go to https://code.jquery.com/ for more details -->
    <script src="https://code.jquery.com/jquery-3.2.1.min.js"
integrity="sha256-hwg4gsxgFZhOsEEamdOYGBf13FyQuiTwlAQgxVSNgt4="
crossorigin="anonymous"></script>
    <script>
    $(document).ready(() => {
        const first_name = "kent";
        const last_name = "clark";
        const addresses = ["5400 W Parmer Ln", "1919 Elridge Pkwy"];
        const zipcodes = ["78757", "77887"];
        const classes = ["International Business", "Economics Statistics"];
        $.ajax({
            "url": "http://localhost:3300/addUser",
            "type": "POST",
            "data": {
                "first_name": first_name,
                "last_name": last_name,
                "addresses": addresses,
                "zip_codes": zipcodes,
```

```
                "classes": classes
            },
            "content-type": "application/json; charset.utf-8",
            "dataType": "JSON"
        }).done(function(data) {
            console.log(data);
        });
    });
    </script>
</head>
<body>
    <h2>Adding a student</h2>
    <p>Storing the student information</p>
</body>
</html>
```

In this call, we are doing multiple things; we start by declaring a few variables to hold local data. We have local variables that hold string values for the first name and last name of the student, and we also have variables that are holding arrays for classes, ZIP codes, and addresses, as Superman has to be at multiple locations in a few minutes. In our AJAX call, the first change to note is the type property; as we are pushing a large amount of user data, it is common to use the HTTP POST method. The data property is going to use the local variables that are declared for the first name, last name, addresses, ZIP codes, and the classes. From the API, when a user is added to the database successfully, we send a list of students in the response, and that will be logged to our **Console** window.

Now, to verify that the new 'student' has been added to our database, we can either check the response of the last array element or run our getStudents API call to see a list of all the users.

The last student in the students feed is 'Kent Clark'; it is always important to test our code to see that everything is working as expected. As we are dealing with dynamic data, it is very important to maintain data integrity. Whenever a CRUD operation is performed on a user or on their dependencies, a verification of data integrity on that data storage has to be performed by looking at the retrieved data and by performing data validation checks.

The problem with cross-domain AJAX calls

All the asynchronous calls that we have made until now have been on the node server. The node server has already handled the functionality for supporting CORS. There are situations where we want to load data from a different domain, such as fetching data from other APIs, which may not have CORS supports. Server-side programs are designed to handle these kinds of call; we can use cURL to make HTTP calls to different domains to fetch such data. This increases our dependency on server-side programs as we have to make a call to our server, which in turn makes a call to another domain to fetch the data, which is returned to a client-side program. It might come across as being a trivial issue, but we are adding an extra layer to our web architecture. To avoid making a server-side call, let us try and see if we can make an asynchronous call to a different domain. For this example, let us use our student JSON API to fetch the data.

As we have already handled the **CORS** on the node server, we need to make following changes in `app.js` in our Node server project:

```
res.writeHead(200, {
    "Content-Type": "application/json",
    //"Access-Control-Allow-Origin" : "*"
});
```

In the preceding snippet we commented the option of `Access-Control-Allow-origin` for simulating unhandled cross-origin resource requests. Once done, run the HTML code shown as follows:

```html
<!--get-student-cor.html-->
<!DOCTYPE html>
<html>
<head>
    <title>Get all students</title>
    <!-- Go to https://code.jquery.com/ for more details -->
    <script
src="https://code.jquery.com/jquery-3.2.1.min.js"
integrity="sha256-hwg4gsxgFZhOsEEamdOYGBf13FyQuiTwlAQgxVSNgt4="
crossorigin="anonymous"></script>
    <script>
    $(document).ready(() => {
        $.ajax({
            "url" : "http://localhost:3300",
            "type" : "GET",
            "data" : {},
            "dataTYPE":"JSON"
        })
        .done((data)=>{
```

```
            console.log(data);
        })
    })
    </script>
</head>
<body>
    <h2>Asynchrnous call for student api</h2>
    <p>Cross origin request neither handled at server not at client
side</p>
</body>
</html>
```

Let's take a look at the output that is generated when we make this asynchronous call across domains:

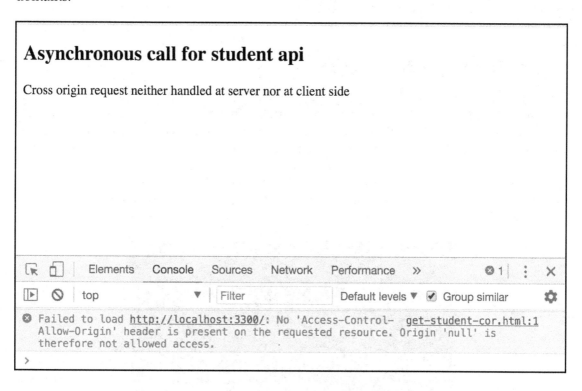

In our asynchronous call, we see an error in the **Console** window. The error says that the XMLHTTPRequest object cannot load the URL that we have provided as it doesn't originate from our browser's current domain, causing us to violate the origin policy. The same domain policy is a security measure followed by web browsers in order to prevent one domain from accessing information on another domain. Web applications use cookies to store basic information about a user's session so as to provide an intuitive user experience when the user requests the same web page another time or requests a different web page on the same domain. To prevent an external website from stealing this information, web browsers follow the same origin policy.

The same domain policy looks for three things in an incoming request; they are the host, the port, and the protocol. To mitigate such issues here is a way to handle CORs known as JSONP. Let's study it in the upcoming section.

Introduction to JSONP

In order to get around the same origin policy, we will be using **JSONP (JSON with Padding)**. One exception under the same origin policy is the <script> tag, so scripts can be passed across domains. JSONP uses this exception in order to pass data across domains as a script by adding padding to make the JSON object look like a script. In JavaScript, when a function with a parameter is invoked, we call the function and add a parameter. With JSONP, we pass the JSON feed as a parameter to a function; thereby, we pad our object into a function callback. This function into which the JSON feed has been padded has to be used on the client-side to retrieve the JSON feed. Let's take a quick look at a JSONP example:

```
untitled

1
2   myCallback({
3       "studentid": "101",
4       "firstname": "John",
5       "lastname": "Doe",
6       "classes": [
7           "Business Research",
8           "Economics",
9           "Finance"
10      ]
11  });
12
```

In this example, we are padding the students object into the `myCallback` function and we have to reuse the `myCallback` function in order to retrieve the students object. Now that we understand how JSONP works, let's use this technique in our application. To incorporate the JSONP solution we also need the support of our server-side code as well. Let's take a look at changes required on the server side in the following section.

Implementation at server-side

To handle a JSONP request, consider the following procedure we need to implement on the server side:

1. Add one more case in our switch block that represents a JSONP request. To do so, consider the following code:

```
case '/.jsonp':
break;
```

2. Once we have our route case ready, the first thing to do is to implement the query parsing logic. In our case, we have already done this operation by using the `querystring.parse` method to parse the query object. This will get the callback details passed as a query parameter from the URL. Next, we need to create a JSONP response as shown in the preceding section. We need first to stringify the JSON response and then pad it into a JSONP callback received from our client:

```
case '/.jsonp':
//validate query parameter
const jsonpCallback  = queryObject.jsonp;
if(!jsonpCallback){
   return res.end(studentsData);
};
let start = jsonpCallback + '(', end = ')';
let stringifiedStudentData = JSON.stringify
(studentsData, undefined, 2);
res.end(start + stringifiedStudentData + end);
break;
```

The preceding code provides the query URL `http://localhost:3300/.jsonp?jsonp=getStudentData`, which when hit in the browser provides a JSONP response. Let us go through the browser-side implementation.

Implementing JSONP at client-side (browsers)

Let's replace the URL property in our earlier script with a newly created script that will fetch the JSON feed. A few properties such as the URL and `dataType` have been modified and a few new properties such as `contentType` and `jsonpCallback` have been added. We have already discussed the change in the URL property, so let us look at the other properties:

```html
<!DOCTYPE html>
<html>
<head>
    <title>Asynchronous Call to Reddit</title>
    <script src="https://code.jquery.com/jquery-3.2.1.min.js"
integrity="sha256-hwg4gsxgFZhOsEEamdOYGBf13FyQuiTwlAQgxVSNgt4="
crossorigin="anonymous"></script>
    <script>
    $(document).ready(() => {
        $.ajax({
                "url": "http://localhost:3300/.jsonp?jsonp=getStudentData",
                "type": "GET",
                "data": {},
                "dataType": "JSONP",
                "jsonpCallback": "getStudentData"
            })
            .done((data) => {
                console.log(data);
            })
    })
    </script>
</head>
<body>
    <h2>Asynchronous call for Students api</h2>
    <p>Cross request is not handled at server but at client</p>
</body>
</html>
```

Earlier, the `dataType` property was set to JSON as the incoming feed was of type JSON, but now the JSON feed is being padded into a callback, and it has to be switched so that the browser expects a callback rather than JSON itself. The new properties that have been added are `contentType` and `jsonpCallback`; the property `contentType` specifies the type of content being sent to the web server . `jsonpCallback` takes the name of the callback function into which the JSON feed has been padded.

When the script is fired, the data from the `getStudentData` callback is retrieved and passed over into the success property that logs our JSON object onto the **Console** window. The output is as shown next:

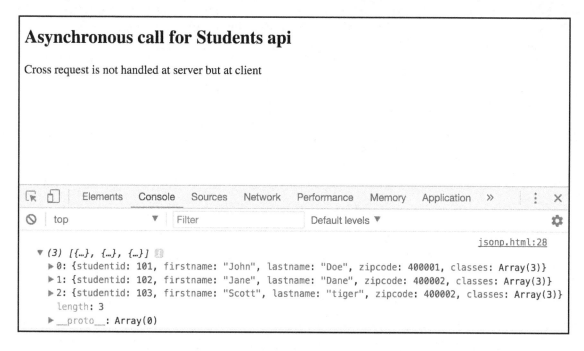

 An important fact to note is that a JSONP call is a script call and not an XHR request, so the JSONP call will be available in the JS or `<scripts>` tab and not in the XHR tab of the **Console** window. Another point to remember is JSON always a `GET` method request.

Summary

HTTP GET and POST request methods are two of the most popular HTTP methods that are used to transfer data from clients to servers. This chapter provides an in-depth understanding of how the GET and POST request methods are used to transfer data using asynchronous requests. We then proceeded to look at cross-origin resource issues and how can we resolve them. Next, we studied the JSONP implementation on the client-side as well as on the server-side.

Concerning cross-domain asynchronous requests, we used the exception of the <script> tag to perform our JSONP asynchronous script calls to fetch the data from a different domain. In the next chapter, we will be learning about debugging JSON using various client-side tools.

Debugging JSON

5

JSON has grown in leaps and bounds in the last few years, and so there is an abundance of freely available resources to help us understand the JSON object we are working with. As we discussed earlier, JSON can be used for multiple purposes, and it is important to understand the simple things that might break JSON, such as ignoring double quotes, a trailing comma on the last item in a JSON object, or the wrong content-type being sent over by the web server. In this chapter, let's go over the different ways in which we can:

- Get acquainted with the dev tools quickly!
- Validate JSON
- Format JSON using some websites

Using the developer tools

Almost all the top browsers, such as Mozilla Firefox, Google Chrome, Safari, and Internet Explorer, have powerful debugging tools that help us understand the requests that are being made, and the responses that are coming back. JSON could either be part of the request, or be part of the response. Google Chrome, Safari, and newer versions of Internet Explorer are shipped with built-in developer tools. Firebug was a very popular web development toolkit that was available for Mozilla Firefox. Firebug is an external plugin and it has to be installed on the browser; it is one of the earliest web development toolkits and was built to assist web developers while using Firefox. Recently, Mozilla Firefox launched new frontend development tools that not only provide the whole development toolkit, but also an environment, by presenting the Firefox developers edition.

 Please visit `https://goo.gl/ZRXCiP` and click on the **Firefox Developer Edition** button on the landing page.

The Firefox developer browser edition provides access to the HTML DOM tree and it gives us a real-time understanding of how the HTML elements are arranged on the page. This browser provides a pack of various DevTools that stimulate web development at client side. Some of the features are listed as follows:

- **Online inspector**: It inspects HTML, CSS, and also JS code online with ease.
- **Javascript debuggers**: They are built with latest tools such as Redux and React.
- **The Network tab**: It allows us to keep track of all resources such as images, JavaScript files, CSS files, flash media, and any asynchronous calls that the client is making. It also monitors latency.
- **The Console window**: It is another popular feature that is built into the developer tools. As the name suggests, this window provides us with a runtime JavaScript console to test any on-the-fly scripts.

To load the developer tools on Firefox developer edition, Google Chrome, and Safari, right-click on a web page and click on **Inspect Element** from the list of options.

When working on Safari, keep in mind that the developer tools have to be enabled; to enable the developer tools:

1. Click on the Safari menu item
2. Choose **Preferences** and click on the **Advanced** tab
3. Check **Show develop menu** in the menu bar to view the developer tools

In Internet Explorer, hit the *F12* key on your keyboard to fire up the developer tools window. In Chapter 3, *AJAX Requests with JSON*, we made our first asynchronous call to a live web server to request JSON data using jQuery. We will be debugging those static HTML files in the Firefox developer edition browser.

To get started we need Node server so that our jQuery Ajax call in the client side script can receive data. Start it using the following command in the node-test-app directory presented in Chapter 3, *AJAX Requests with JSON*:

```
npm start
```

Let us open jquery-ajax.html in a browser and debug the data using the developer tools; for this example we will be using the Firefox web browser:

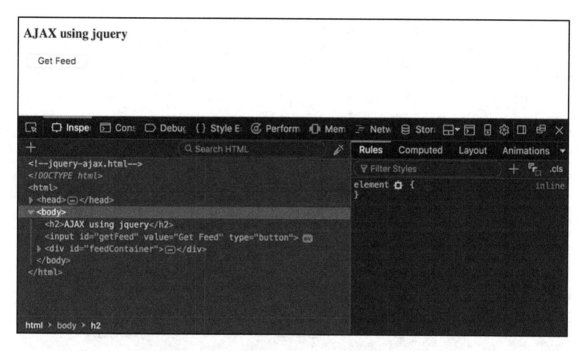

On page load, when a user right-clicks and chooses **Inspect Element**, the **html** tab is loaded up by default and the user gets to see the HTML DOM. In our example, we bound a click event handler to the **Get Feed** button. Let us look at the **Console** output after the button was clicked; to view the output in the **Console** window, click on the **Console** tab:

Once the response is retrieved, the JSON feed is logged into the **Console** window. Throughout this book, we have extensively used the `console.log` method to print the data onto the **Console** window, which is a helpful feature of the developer tools. It is important to understand the JSON feed that is parsed and displayed. Also, the developer tools' **Console** window provides us with a simple way to analyze the JSON feed. Let's continue our research on the developer tools and visit the **Network** tab in Firefox, to understand how the client and the server communicate the content type of the data that the client is expecting:

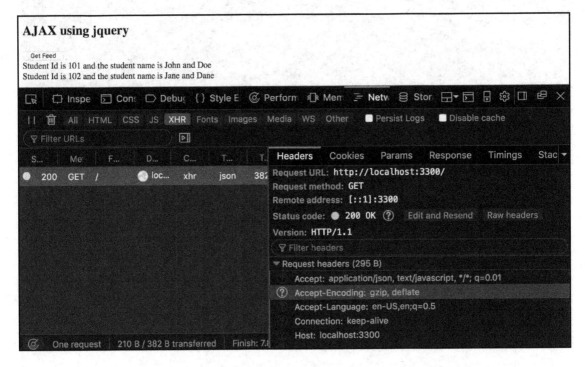

In the net window, we should begin by clicking on the URL for the asynchronous call, which is being made to `http://localhost:3300/`. Once that link is clicked, in the **Headers** section we should observe the `Accept` header, which is expecting the `application/json`. We also need to take note that there are two requests on the left-hand column. One is a script request and the other is `XHR` or `XMLHttpRequest`, which notifies that this is an asynchronous request. The **Response** tab on the right of the **Network** window will display the JSON feed for this request.

Validating JSON

Similar to our debugging resources, there are a lot of popular web tools that help us validate JSON that were building. JSONLint is one of the most popular web tools that are available for validate our JSON feeds.

 To work with JSONLint, please visit https://jsonlint.com/.

JSONLint has a very straightforward interface that allows the user to paste the JSON they want to validate, and returns either a success message or an error message based on the JSON feed that we paste. Let us begin by validating a bad piece of JSON to see the error message returned, and then let us fix it to view the success message.

For this example, I will copy the students feed from the previous example, and add a trailing comma at the end of the second element:

```
C  🔒 Secure  https://jsonlint.com                                            Q  ☆  ⟲  ▲  ⊘
Apps  For quick access, place your bookmarks here on the bookmarks bar.  Import bookmarks now...

 1 ▾ [{
 2        "studentid": 101,
 3        "firstname": "John",
 4        "lastname": "Doe",
 5 ▾      "classes": ["Business Research", "Economics", "Finance"]
 6 ▾ }, {
 7        "studentid": 102,
 8        "firstname": "Jane",
 9        "lastname": "Dane",
10 ▾      "classes": ["Marketing", "Economics", "Finance"]
11    }, ]
```

Validate JSON   **Clear**   Support JSONLint for $2/Month

Results

```
Error: Parse error on line 11:
...ics", "Finance"]}, ]
--------------------^
Expecting 'STRING', 'NUMBER', 'NULL', 'TRUE', 'FALSE', '{', '[', got ']'
```

Notice that we have added a trailing comma to the last item in our JSON object, and the best part about JSONLint is the descriptive error message. We have encountered a `Parse error`, and to make life simple the message also gives us the line number where the error could be. The parser is expecting a string, a number, a null, or a Boolean value, and because we have supplied none, we encounter this error. In order to fix this error, we will either have to add a new item to that JSON object to justify the comma, or we will have to get rid of the comma, as there are no items ahead:

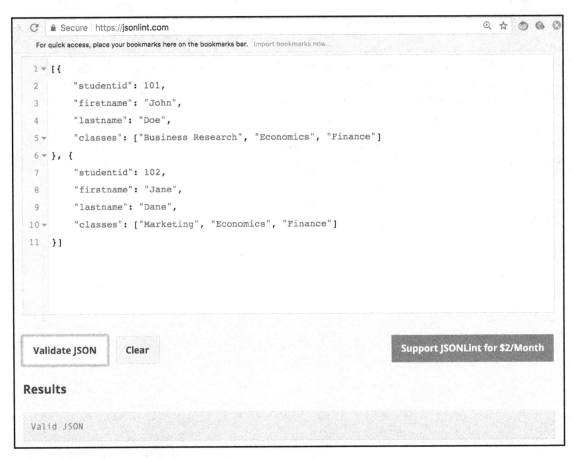

As soon as we remove the trailing comma and validate it, we get the success message. Ease of use and descriptive messages have made JSONLint one of the go-to websites for JSON validation.

Formatting JSON

JSONLint is not just an online JSON validator, it also helps us format JSON and makes it look pretty. Often JSON feeds are big, and an online editor that provides a tree structure to traverse through JSON objects is always helpful. JSON Editor Online is one of my favorite online editors to work with and format big JSON objects, as it provides an easy-to-navigate tree structure:

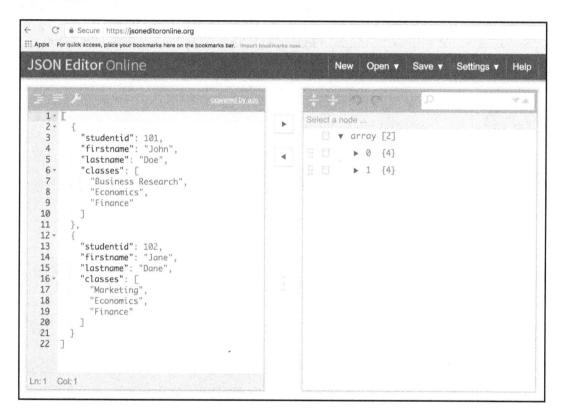

 To work with JSON Editor Online, please visit `https://jsoneditoronline.org/.`

We begin by pasting our JSON example code into the window on the left-hand side, and click on the right arrow button in the middle to generate our tree structure. Once we make changes to the tree structure, we can click on the left arrow button to format our data, making it ready to use elsewhere.

Summary

Debugging, validating, and formatting are three things that developers can never ignore. In this chapter, we have looked at resources such as developer toolkits for browsers, which we can use for debugging and, how we can utilize these developer toolkits; we also saw how to use JSONLint for validation and JSON Editor Online for formatting.

This is the end of JavaScript and JSON Essentials, targeted to provide you with an in-depth insight into how data can be stored and transferred in the JSON data format. We have had hands-on experience of transferring JSON via HTTP asynchronous requests within the same domain and HTTP asynchronous requests across domains. We have also looked at alternative implementations of how the JSON data format can be used. This is a solid start to a long journey towards understanding JSON to develop interactive and responsive web applications. In Chapter 6, *Building the Carousel Application*, we are going to actually apply all the frontend side scripting knowledge that we have learned so far to developing a Carousel application.

6
Building the Carousel Application

We have come a long way in our journey to master JavaScript and JSON; it is now time to get busy and build an end-to-end project that is powered by JSON. In our journey, we have come across a variety of concepts such as JavaScript, JSON, the use of server-side programming, AJAX, and JSONP. So, let's put all of these to use. In this chapter, we will be focusing on the application of what we learned in previous chapters:

- Setting up an application
- Introducing Bootstrap
- Moving towards maintaining the JSON store
- Implementing Carousel functionality using jQuery Cycle

We will be building a rotating notification board application, which should display the top students for the month. This application should provide Carousel functionality, such as navigational buttons, autoplay of content, displaying a single item at a given point, and keeping track of the first and last piece of content.

Setting up the Carousel application

Let's begin by building a folder that will hold the files for this application. This application will need an HTML file that will hold the Carousel; it will need a few libraries such as jQuery and jQuery Cycle; we will have to import these libraries. We also need a JSON file that holds the data for this exercise. To download the jQuery file, please visit `https://jquery.com`. As we have already observed, jQuery is the most popular JavaScript library available to developers. There is a growing community of developers who make jQuery more popular by the day. We will be using the jQuery Cycle library to power our Carousel application. jQuery Cycle is one of the most popular and lightweight cycle libraries with numerous features such as responsive components, configuration-based interactivity for next, previous button, throttle speed, and so on. it can be downloaded from `http://malsup.github.io/jquery.cycle.all.js` directly. Rename the file to `jquery.cycle.js` as we are using that name.

Create a directory named `chapter 6` and store all the downloaded files in it. We are planning for the following structure:

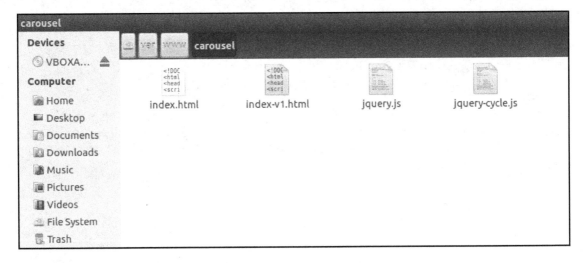

Now that we have the libraries arranged in the document root, let's work on the basic HTML file that will import these files into the web page, as shown in the following snippet:

```
//index.html
<!DOCTYPE html>
<html>
<head>
    <script type="text/javascript" src="jquery-3.2.1.min.js"></script>
    <script type="text/javascript" src="jquery.cycle.js"></script>
```

```
    <script type="text/javascript">
    $(document).ready(() => {
        console.log("Ready!");
    })
    </script>
</head>
<body>
</body>
</html>
```

This is our initial index web page, which will load the JavaScript files onto the web page. When this file is fired up via a web browser, both JavaScript libraries have to be loaded and ready and should be printed onto the console window. Now, let's move forward and build our Carousel application. Next in the line of requirements is the data file; it will be similar to the students JSON feed that we have worked with in our previous chapters. Rather than printing them all in a single line, we will be loading them into a rotator application.

Building the JSON file for the Carousel application

Let's assume that we are an educational institution, and we have a tradition of acknowledging the efforts of our students on a monthly basis. We will pick the top students from each course for that month, and display their names on our notice board rotator application. This notice board rotator application has often served as a motivation for other students, who always aim to get themselves onto that board. This is the way our educational institution encourages the students to do well in their courses. The example JSON feed will look as follows:

```
students.json        x      data-example1.json  ●      index-v1.html       x
1
2    {
3        "studentid": "101",
4        "firstname": "John",
5        "lastname": "Doe",
6        "level": "Freshman",
7        "class": "Environmental Toxicology"
8    },
9    |
```

For our notice board rotator application, we will need basic student information, such as the first name, last name, current level of education, and the course that they have excelled in:

```
<script type="text/javascript">
$(document).ready(()=>{
    $.getJSON('http://localhost:3000', (data)=>{
        console.log("data on ", data);
    })
})
</script>
```

In the preceding snippet, we are using jQuery's `getJSON()` function to bring the JSON feed into the document. When the `index.html` file is loaded into the browser, the students JSON object array will be loaded onto the console window. It is about time to start extracting data from the JSON object, and to start embedding it onto the DOM. Let's use the jQuery `each()` function to loop over the students, JSON feed and load the data onto the page.

The `each()` function in jQuery is similar to the `foreach()` iterative loop, which is available with popular server-side languages, and the `for in()` iterative loop, which is available in the native JavaScript. The `each()` iterator takes the data as its first argument, and passes each item in that data iteratively as a single key-value pair into a callback. This callback is a collection of a number of scripts that are executed on that key-value pair. In this callback, we are building the HTML file that will be appended to a `div` element on the DOM. We are using this callback to iteratively build the HTML file for all the elements that exist in that student's JSON object:

```
<script type="text/javascript">
$(document).ready(() => {
    let htmlContent = ``;
    $.getJSON('http://localhost:3300', (data) => {
        $.each(data, (key, value) => {
            $.each(value, (index, student) => {
                htmlContent += `<div class="student">`;
                htmlContent += `<h3>${student.level} of the Month</h3>`;
                htmlContent += `<h4>${student.firstname}
${student.lastname}</h4>`;
                htmlContent += `<p>${student.class}</p>`;
                htmlContent += `</div>`;
            });
        });
        $('#students').html(htmlContent)
    })
})
</script>
```

In the `index.html` file, we are using the jQuery `each()` function to iterate through the student's JSON feed, and build the HTML file that will display the student information, such as the first name, last name, the year of college, and the course that they are enrolled in. We are building the dynamic HTML and assigning it to the HTML variable. The data in the `html` variable will be added later to the `div` element with an ID of students. This is shown in the following HTML code:

```html
<body>
<div id="students"></div>
</body>
```

The following screenshot shows the output of the `index.html` body:

Freshman of the Month

John Doe

Environmental Toxicology

Senior of the Month

Jane Dane

Economics

expert of the Month

Scott tiger

Physics

When the script is loaded into a web browser, the script checks to see whether the document is ready. Once the document is ready, an AJAX call is made to the server to retrieve the JSON data. Once the JSON data is retrieved, each object in the students JSON object array feed will be passed into the callback that generates an HTML `div` element with a class student. This repeats until the callback is run on the last element; once the callback is executed on the last element, this HTML file will be appended to a `div` element in the HTML with an ID of students.

Now as with respect to the improvisation of code, we can make a small change in the way the HTML is appended to the `htmlContent` variable. This can be done as follows:

```
$.each(data, (index, student)=>{
htmlContent+=`<div class="student">
<h3>${student.level} of the Month</h3>
<h4>${student.firstname} ${student.lastname}</h4>
<p>${student.class}</p>
</div>`;
});
```

If we compare this script we studied earlier, instead of performing the appending operation for every HTML statement differently, we can add it using the back quote or back-tick key (`) and perform a single operation. This provides optimization benefits. Once done, the next step is to add the slide-show functionality using jQuery Cycle, which is explained in the following section.

Creating the Carousel application with jQuery Cycle

We have developed a web page that loads all the student data into an HTML file; now it is time to build the Carousel application using this data. We will be using a jQuery Cycle plugin to rotate the student information on our notice board application. jQuery Cycle is a slideshow plugin that supports various types of transition effects on multiple browsers. Effects such as fade, toss, wipe, zoom, scroll, and shuffle are available. The plugin also supports the pause action on the hover of the slide as a feature; click triggers and response callbacks are also supported.

For our Carousel example, let's keep it simple and use the basic options, such as a fade effect to rotate the students, enabling the pause so that, whenever a user hovers over the cycle, the rotator application is paused to display the information of the current student. Finally, we will be setting the speed and the timeout values that will determine how much time it will take to transition from one student to another:

```javascript
<script type="text/javascript">
$(document).ready(() => {
    let htmlContent = ``;
    $.getJSON('http://localhost:3300', (data) => {
        console.log("data", data);
        $.each(data, (index, student) => {
            htmlContent += `<div class="student">
          <div class="col-lg-12 text-center">
            <h3>${student.level} of the Month</h3>

            <h4 class="lead">${student.firstname} ${student.lastname}</h4>

            <p>${student.class}</p>
          </div>
        </div>`;
        });
        $('#students').html(htmlContent);

        $('#students').cycle({
            "cleartypeNoBg": true,
            "fx": "fade",
            "pause": "1",
            "prev": "#prev",
            "next": "#next",
            "speed": 500,
            "timeout": 10000
        })
    })
})
</script>
```

In the preceding snippet, we set up the cycle plugin, and added it to the `div` element of the students. The cycle plugin takes a JSON object as its parameter, to add the rotator functionality to a `div` element. In this JSON object, we have added four properties: `fx`, `pause`, `speed`, and `timeout`. `fx` determines the effect that is performed on the HTML element. `fade` is a prominent effect that is used for the Cycle plugin. The other popular effects that are supported by the jQuery Cycle plugin are `shuffle`, `zoom`, `turndown`, `scrollRight`, and `curtainX`. The second property we are using is the `pause` property, which determines whether the rotation has stopped when the user hovers over the rotator element; it takes a true and false value to determine if the rotation can be paused or not. We could either supply a Boolean value such as `true` or `false`, or pass one or zero to signify True and False, respectively. The next two properties are speed and timeout; they determine the speed with which the rotation occurs and how much time it will take before the next item is displayed. When the web page with the updated script is loaded into a web browser, the whole students object is parsed into a local JavaScript string variable and is appended to the DOM, and only the first element in that rotator object is displayed while the rest of them are hidden. This functionality is handled behind-the-scenes by the Cycle plugin. The following screenshot displays a Carousel generated from the earlier code sample:

Freshman of the Month

John Doe

Environmental Toxicology

Let's enhance the user experience of this page by adding earlier handlers and those in the following code to give the users custom controllers to handle the rotator functionality, as shown in the following snippet:

```
<!DOCTYPE html>
<html>
<head>
<script type="text/javascript" src="jquery-3.2.1.min.js"></script>
<script type="text/javascript" src="jquery.cycle.js"></script>\
<script type="text/javascript">
$(document).ready((()=>{
```

```
let htmlContent = ``;
$.getJSON('http://localhost:3300', (data)=>{
console.log("data", data);
$.each(data, (index, student)=>{
htmlContent+=`<div class="student">
<h3>${student.level} of the Month</h3>`;
htmlContent +=`<h4>${student.firstname} ${student.lastname}</h4>`;
htmlContent+=`<p>${student.class}</p>`;
htmlContent+=`</div>`;
});
$('#students').html(htmlContent);
$('#students').cycle({
"cleartypeNoBg" : true,
"fx" : "fade",
"pause" : "1",
"prev" : "#prev",
"next" : "#next",
"speed" : 500,
"timeout" : 10000
})
})
})
</script>
</head>
<body>
<a href="#" id="prev">Prev</a>
<a href="#" id="next">Next</a>
<div id="students"></div>
</body>
</html>
```

In the preceding snippet, we have added two anchor element with ID values of prev and next ; these are referenced in the cycle object.

In the cycle object, we are adding two new properties called prev and next. The values for the prev and next properties will be the HTML ID attributes of elements that are on the DOM.

The **Prev** and **Next** links that are shown in the preceding screenshot are going to handle the rotation of our notice board rotation application:

```
Prev Next

expert of the Month

Scott tiger

Physics
```

This is a quick way of building a Carousel application that is powered by jQuery and JSON. This example can be used to build more complex Carousel applications that can contain images and videos for photo and video gallery Carousel applications, respectively.

Introducing Bootstrap

Our Carousel application is working fluently. The only thing is that the applications look too subtle and non-intuitive. To help us add some look and feel characteristics to our application, Bootstrap comes to the rescue.

> *Bootstrap is a free and open-source frontend web framework for designing websites and web applications.*

> *–en.wikipedia.org*

All UI components such as tabs, modals, lists, and so on, which are required to complete the designing or GUI part of an application, are already contained in Bootstrap. The developer needs to tweak some elements and change the CSS properties to build a customized one. Let's implement Bootstrap in our Carousel applications.

Setting up Bootstrap

Bootstrap provides an easy way to set up its libraries for your application. Like any other third-party library, we can provide a **content delivery network** (**CDN**) link directly or can download the file.

Bootstrap also contains JavaScript links for user interface interactions and events, but in our application we only need the CSS.

So here is the link that needs to be placed inside the head tag. This can be used as follows:

```
<link rel="stylesheet" type="text/css" href="
https://maxcdn.bootstrapcdn.com/bootstrap/4.0.0-beta.2/css/bootstrap.min.cs
s">
```

We download the CSS file from the preceding link for our application, so that readers can refer to it even if they are offline or without an internet connection.

Once downloaded it will be named bootstrap.min.css, and stored in our respective application directory. This can be linked to our HTML file as follows:

```
<link rel="stylesheet" type="text/css" href="bootstrap.min.css">
```

To check whether the preceding CSS file is successfully linked, we need to load our application in the browser. The following screenshot shows successful Bootstrap stylesheet linking:

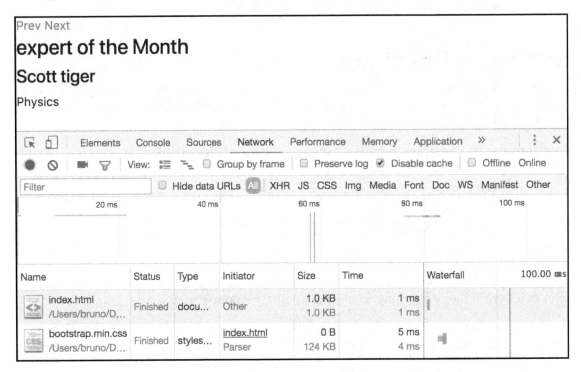

The **Status** tab in the preceding screenshot has a **Finished** status, which means the CSS file loaded successfully.

The next step is to implement some layout styles.

Bootstrap responsiveness and styles

Let's go through the steps to style our app, starting with layout elements and then targeting specific ones:

1. To add layout styles we need to add the magic class called `container`. Why is it magic? Because it is responsible for handling the layout of the web application for each device. This class should be added to the parent of all the elements. The application that we are building has a `div` element immediately after the body element. And that's the parent to all the Carousel elements:

   ```
   <div id="students" class="container"></div>
   ```

It a good practice to not include body elements as a container, as later it may create limitations on designing more parent blocks.

By adding the `container` class, we get the following output:

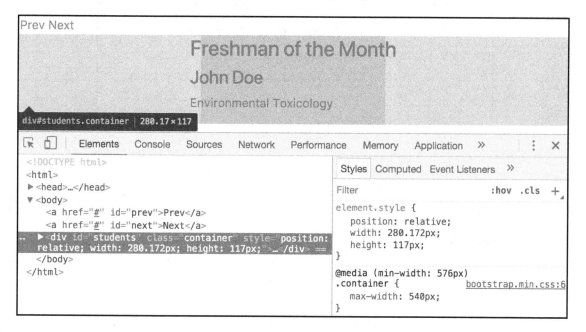

2. Once `container` is applied we need to implement the grid system of Bootstrap. The Bootstrap grid system consists of one single row class with multiple column classes. The columns can be divided further into twelve sub-columns. In our case, we are just going to add everything in one row and a single column. As our inner content is dynamically loaded in the parent `div`, we need to make changes in jQuery's each loop callback, which is done as follows:

```
$.each(data, (index, student) => {
    htmlContent += `<div class="student">
      <div class="col-lg-12 text-center">
        <h3>${student.level} of the Month</h3>
        <h4 class="lead">${student.firstname}
        ${student.lastname}</h4>
        <p>${student.class}</p>
      </div>
    </div>`;
});
```

This gives us the following output:

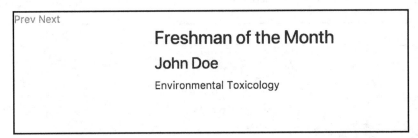

3. Now the layout looks conventional, let's focus on individual elements. We are going to provide a Bootstrap feel to the following elements:
   - Navigation buttons
   - Carousel text

To accumulate all the changes, here is the final HTML template:

```
<!DOCTYPE html>
<html>

<head>
    <link rel="stylesheet" type="text/css" href="bootstrap.min.css">
    <script type="text/javascript" src="jquery-3.2.1.min.js"></script>
    <script type="text/javascript" src="jquery.cycle.js"></script>
    <script type="text/javascript">
    $(document).ready(() => {
```

```
            let htmlContent = ``;
            $.getJSON('http://localhost:3300', (data) => {
                console.log("data", data);
                $.each(data, (index, student) => {
                    htmlContent += `<div class="student">
<div class="col-lg-12 text-center">
<h3>${student.level} of the Month</h3>
<h4 class="lead">${student.firstname} ${student.lastname}</h4>
<p>${student.class}</p>
</div>
</div>`;
                });
                $('#students').html(htmlContent);
                $('#students').cycle({
                    "cleartypeNoBg": true,
                    "fx": "fade",
                    "pause": "1",
                    "prev": "#prev",
                    "next": "#next",
                    "speed": 500,
                    "timeout": 10000
                })
            })
        })
    </script>
</head>
<style type="text/css">
.btn-left {
    position: absolute;
    left: 20px;
    top: 10%;
}

.btn-right {
    position: absolute;
    right: 20px;
    top: 10%;
}
</style>

<body>
    <a href="#" id="prev" class="btn btn-primary btn-left">Prev</a>
    <a href="#" id="next" class="btn btn-primary btn-right">Next</a>
    <div id="students" class="container"></div>
</body>

</html>
```

The revamped template is shown in the following screenshot:

Woot! Our Carousel application is completed. Our JSON journey has now completed a milestone: implementing an application at the frontend. In upcoming chapters, we are going to explore alternate implementations of JSON data on the server-side and client-side as well.

Summary

In this chapter, we put our JavaScript, jQuery, and JSON knowledge to work, and built up a neat little Carousel notice board rotator application. We went through a step-by-step process to ingest the data feed, build a dynamic template on-the-fly from that data feed, append the data feed to a `div` element, and then bind the `div` element to the cycle plugin. This notice board rotator application gives us an insight into bigger Carousel projects that can be developed with very little development effort. Finally, we revamped our application by using Bootstrap and learned how it can be implemented for different UI building blocks in our app. In the next chapter, we will look at alternative implementations of JSON.

7
Alternate Implementations of JSON

So far, we have worked with JSON as an HTTP data interchange format; now let's look at popular alternative methods in which JSON is being used. In the last few years, there has been a sharp rise in the number of software modules and packages across all programming and scripting languages.

In this chapter, we are going to learn the following implementations of JSON:

- Dependency management in PHP and Node.js
- JSON for storing application configurations in PHP and Angular
- Application metadata in Angular
- Constants in Node.js
- JSON metadata usage for embedding templates or so-called server-side rendering

Scripting languages such as PHP or JavaScript have a huge number of contributed software packages and modules. The advantage here is using a prebuilt software package that provides certain functionality out of the box and has been heavily tested by the community. The flip side of introducing a single framework or multiple frameworks into a software project is having to understand how these frameworks are loaded into the project, how they can be accessed from different sections in the current project, whether these frameworks have any dependencies, and finally how they affect the whole project. These issues can be addressed by using a **dependency manager**.

Dependency management

A dependency manager is a software program that keeps track of all the necessary base programs that are required for a dependent program to run. A common practice in a software development life cycle is to perform unit tests by using a unit-testing framework; the unit-testing framework in turn might need some base libraries to be installed or there might be a few settings to enable the use of that framework.

These operations are often handled by writing up quick scripts, but as the project grows, the dependencies grow along with the project. Along the same lines, tracking these changes and making sure different teams working on the project get the relevant updates, which is done by scripts, is a tough task. By introducing a dependency manager, we will be automating the whole process, which adds consistency and saves time.

Using composer.json in PHP

Dependency management has often been a little rocky, and for new developers who are just coming in adding new frameworks into their projects, setting up their projects, and getting them to run can be daunting. A dependency manager such as Composer for PHP solves this issue. It is considered as the "glue between all projects," and there is a good reason for that. Composer uses JSON to keep track of all the dependencies for a given project. Composer's primary job is to download libraries from remote locations and store them locally. To inform Composer as to what libraries we need, we need to set up the `composer.json` file. This file keeps track of all the specific libraries, their versions, and the environments that a given library should be deployed to. For example, a unit-testing framework library should never make it to production. There was an instance where a colleague of mine who was randomly testing our production instance deleted the whole user table by running a unit test; we had to recover the whole user table from the previous night's database back ups.

Let's quickly dive in and see how JSON is used to handle dependency management:

```
composer.json        x
1
2    {
3
4         "require":{
5              "php": ">=5.4.7"
6         },
7         "require-dev":{
8              "phpunit/phpunit": "3.7.*"
9         }
10
11   }
12
```

In the `composer.json` file, we are adding two requirements to install a specific version of PHP and PHPUnit. Once the files are added to the project, we can use Composer's `install` command to install these dependencies. Composer also comes with an `update` command that takes care of any updates for a given package.

 For more information about Composer, please visit: `http://www.getcomposer.org`.

Node.js using the package.json registry

Node.js is a popular software platform that uses the JSON data format for tracking dependencies. The **Node Packaged Modules** (**NPM**) is the package manager that developers use for installing and integrating external modules into their code. For every Node.js project, there is a package.json file in the document root that keeps track of all the metadata, such as the name of the project, the name of the author, the version number, the required modules to run that project, and the underlying daemons or engines that are required to run the project. Let's take a peek at an example package.json file from one of my Node.js projects:

```json
package.json          ×
1
2  {
3      "name": "TestNodeJSProject",
4      "version": "0.0.1",
5      "author": "Sai Sriparasa <sai.sriparasa@test.com>",
6      "dependencies": {
7          "async": "0.1.18",
8          "connect": "1.8.6",
9          "connect-assetmanager": "0.0.27",
10         "connect-auth": "0.5.1",
11         "connect-mongo": "0.1.7",
12         "cron": "0.3.0",
13         "email": "0.2.5",
14         "emailjs": "0.2.8",
15         "express": "2.5.10",
16         "express-form": "0.6.2",
17         "express-messages": "0.0.2",
18         "eyes": "0.1.7",
19         "fbgraph": "0.2.1",
20         "facebook-sdk": "0.3.2",
21         "jade": "0.26.0",
22         "moment": "1.7.0",
23         "mongodb": "1.0.2",
24      },
25      "engines": {"node": "0.6.x", "npm": "1.0.x"}
26  }
```

The `package.json` file is a big JSON object that keeps track of metadata, such as the project's name, author details, and the required modules.

> For more information about NPM, please visit: `https://www.npmjs.org`.

JSON for storing application configurations

Prior to JSON becoming popular, configurations were either stored in a text file or in language-specific files, such as `config.php` for PHP, `config.py` for Python, and `config.js` for JavaScript. All these can now be replaced by a language-independent `config.json` file; use a JSON library for non-JavaScript libraries to parse it.

Configuration in PHP and Python

Let's take a quick look at an example `config.json` file:

```json
config.json          x      schema.json        x
1
2   {
3
4       "PROJECT":"test project",
5       "ENV":"DEV",
6       "AUTOLOAD":[
7                   "class1.php",
8                   "class2.php",
9                   "class3.php"
10          ],
11      "EXCLUDE":[
12                  "project_x",
13                  "vendor"
14          ],
15      "RECURSIVE":"true"
16
17  }
18
```

In the `config.json` file, we store the metadata as a JSON object. We are specifying important information such as the project name, the environment of the project (which varies based on the server that the file is located on), any classes that have to be autoloaded during bootstrapping the application, and any classes or folders that we would want to exclude. Finally, using the `RECURSIVE` key, we also specify that there are folders and those folders have files.

 Bootstrapping is the startup process for an application, in which we prepare that application to serve its purpose.

Once we have the `config.json` file available, we can use the `json.loads` method in Python or we can use the `json_decode` method in PHP to parse through the `config` object to retrieve the data. The JSON objects can also be used to store the database schema; this helps the rest of the development team to update their database schema when one developer on the team makes a change to the database. A smart way to handle this would be by writing a trigger on this `schema.json` file, and if there is an update to that file, the schema in the database has to be updated to reflect the new changes via the database migration scripts. Let's take a quick look at an example `schema.json` file:

```json
{

    "client":{
        "id":{
                "type":"int",
                "size":11,
                "primaryKey":"true",
                "required":"true"
        },
        "name":{
                "type":"varchar",
                "size":255,
                "required":"true"
        },
        "enabled":{
                "type":"tinyint",
                "size":4,
                "required":"true",
                "defaultValue":1
        }
    }

}
```

In the `schema.json` example, we are building the schema JSON object that will store the database schema information. `client` is the name of the table in our schema. The client table has three columns—the ID, name, and status of the client, that is, whether the client is enabled or disabled. Each of the columns contains the column JSON object that provides the schema information, such as the datatype and size of the column and whether it has a default value or a primary key constraint.

Configuration in frontend frameworks – Angular 5

The new Angular framework is a complete set of frontend development tools. It also provides an end to end testing environment using various testing libraries at client side. Formerly known as `angular.js`, it was just a JavaScript library that only provided model-view-controller architecture for mainly browser-based single page applications. The Angular project has been maintained by Google so far. With respect to our context of the section, we are going to start with Angular version 5, which will implicate our study on the implementation of configuration-based JSON.

 In new Angular (version 2 or above), we use TypeScript as the base script language for development purposes. As per TypeScript documentation, it is a language that scales JavaScript with type strict features and it adds more syntactical sugar to code. Further for deployment purpose and browser usage, we can transpile the code to pure JavaScript. The transpiling process compiles the TypeScript code to JavaScript. For more details, check out this link: `https://en.wikipedia.org/wiki/Source-to-source_compiler`.

To understand the configuration as a feature in Angular, we need to set the framework up on our machine. I would recommend our readers to follow the steps provided in the following link to set up an Angular framework: `https://angular.io/guide/quickstart#devenv`.

Once the procedure is complete, the framework provides a scaffolding, which is shown as follows:

The preceding structure of `my-app` is projected using vscode editor by Microsoft. For more details, check out the following link: `https://code.visualstudio.com/`.

All the JSON files are the configuration files required to construct an application in Angular. Let's learn them one by one.

Linting with tslint.json

Linting is the process of checking or debugging some syntactical, styling error of code. The process of linting is essential for code maintainability and readability. Linting can also eliminate some futuristic errors that may give rise to bugs. tslint.json provides the developer to write the project-specific rules using JSON specification structure. You may already have noticed that as the linting configuration is related to TypeScript, it is prefixed as ts.

The following example illustrates some self-explanatory linting rules of my-app from the tslint.json file. Please refer to the following comments to understand it better:

```
{
    "rules":
        {
//short hand arrow return: getData((someVariable)=>someVariable)
        "arrow-return-shorthand": true,
//Indentation of spaces allowed
            "indent": [
                true,
                "spaces"
            ],
//Semicolon after every end of statement neccessary
            "semicolon": [
                true,
                "always"
            ],
  //Conditional operator used for type match : allowed
            "triple-equals": [
                true,
                "allow-null-check"
            ]
        }
}
```

Configuring TypeScript using tsconfig.json

tsconfig is also called the root file of a TypeScript project. It initializes your TypeScript project and uses the specific configuration rules while compiling **ts**. Let us have a look at some important rules and what they are meant for:

```
{
//On saving the ts file, compile the ts to js
    "compileOnSave": true,
    "compilerOptions": {
//Targeting option for ecmascript versions
        "target": "es5",
//Library files that need to be included for target
        "lib": [
            "es2017",
            "dom"
        ]
    }
}
```

The global tsconfig file is inherited using the extend property in a specific source directory 's tsconfig.json.

Check out the following link for more information on each key and its usage: http://json. schemastore.org/tsconfig.

Using package.json and package-lock.json files

We have already studied package.json in the preceding section. To summarize package.json, it is a registry that maintains information about the application such as name, author, test script, and so on, and manages the dependent modules required for production and developmental levels. Recently, NPM provided an update that also produces package-lock.json files initially during package updates or installation.

A glimpse of `package-lock.json` is provided in the following screenshot:

```json
{
    "name": "phonebook-app2",
    "version": "0.0.0",
    "lockfileVersion": 1,
    "requires": true,
    "dependencies": {
        "@angular-devkit/build-optimizer": {
            "version": "0.0.13",
            "resolved": "https://registry.npmjs.org/@angular-devkit/build-optimizer/-/build-op
            "integrity": "sha512-yEMkYU4YU8XLA5OauPhg22ZEWJ4X2VhiFKUwfeo4UWJ7lz4XWiuBJocrTSNHW
            "dev": true,
            "requires": {
                "loader-utils": "1.1.0",
                "source-map": "0.5.7",
                "typescript": "2.3.4"
            }
        },
        "@angular/animations": {
            "version": "4.4.6",
            "resolved": "https://registry.npmjs.org/@angular/animations/-/animations-4.4.6.tgz
            "integrity": "sha1-mYYmaik44y3xYPHpcl85l1ZKjU=",
            "requires": {
                "tslib": "1.8.0"
            }
        },
        "@angular/cli": {
            "version": "1.3.2",
            "resolved": "https://registry.npmjs.org/@angular/cli/-/cli-1.3.2.tgz",
```

The `package-lock.json` file intends to specify all the records of packages that were updated with respect to time. You do not have to visit each and every node module in an application individually to check for its dependency information. This facilitates a tree-like structure for the modules. `package-lock.json` also provides performance benefits during node module installations.

Using the angular-cli.json file

The new Angular leverages **command line interface** (**cli**) for various purposes such as application booting, deployment, or creating components. The command used to perform such tasks are prefixed with the `ng` command. For instance: the `ng serve` command, to compile the code just in time and keep watch on file changes via webpack simultaneously.

Webpack:
An open source tool to create an environment-specific build for JavaScript applications. Check out `https://webpack.js.org/` for more info.

All such operations we perform at application level are configurable via the `angular-cli.json` file. Consider the following screenshot that provides the default settings we receive on installation:

```
{} .angular-cli.json ×
1    {
2        "$schema": "./node_modules/@angular/cli/lib/config/schema.json",
3        "project": {
4            "name": "my-app"
5        },
6        "apps": [
7            {
8                "root": "src",
9                "outDir": "dist",
10               "assets": [
11                   "assets",
12                   "favicon.ico"
13               ],
14               "index": "index.html",
15               "main": "main.ts",
16               "polyfills": "polyfills.ts",
17               "test": "test.ts",
18               "tsconfig": "tsconfig.app.json",
19               "testTsconfig": "tsconfig.spec.json",
20               "prefix": "app",
21               "styles": [
22                   "styles.css"
23               ],
24               "scripts": [],
25               "environmentSource": "environments/environment.ts",
26               "environments": {
27                   "dev": "environments/environment.ts",
28                   "prod": "environments/environment.prod.ts"
```

Note that the `apps` key in `angular-cli.json` consists of an array, which means we can manage multiple apps from multiple sources in Angular scaffoldings. Let us test our settings by running the application using `ng serve --app 0` or simply `ng serve`. We will achieve the following output:

```
Last login: Wed Apr 11 17:14:12 on ttys010
brunos-MacBook-Pro:my-app bruno$ ng serve --app 0
** NG Live Development Server is listening on localhost:4200, open your browser on http://localhost:4200
**
Date: 2018-04-11T16:37:16.281Z
Hash: fd7734d6620b30a52717
Time: 9010ms
chunk {inline} inline.bundle.js, inline.bundle.js.map (inline) 5.83 kB [entry] [rendered]
chunk {main} main.bundle.js, main.bundle.js.map (main) 6.03 kB {vendor} [initial] [rendered]
chunk {polyfills} polyfills.bundle.js, polyfills.bundle.js.map (polyfills) 199 kB {inline} [initial] [ren
dered]
chunk {styles} styles.bundle.js, styles.bundle.js.map (styles) 11.3 kB {inline} [initial] [rendered]
chunk {vendor} vendor.bundle.js, vendor.bundle.js.map (vendor) 2.29 MB [initial] [rendered]

webpack: Compiled successfully.
```

The output states that the code just about compiled successfully.

Now by running the command as `ng built`, the code is compiled with an **ahead of time (AOT)** compiler and a deployment build of the app is created. Consider the following screenshot:

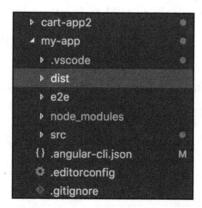

Note that after the process is completed a new directory `dist` is created. This is a deployment-ready code converted to JavaScript. The reason for us to learn about this process is that if we make the changes to the `angular-cli.json` file with key data `"outDir": "dist"` to `"outDir": "distribution"`, it will change the build directory name to `distribution`.

This is one of the outstanding features of new Angular that has fully exploited the features of JSON as configurable. For more details regarding how other keys work in Angular configuration, the team behind Angular has aggregated the CLI module documentation in the form of stories. Check out this link to get more details: `https://github.com/angular/angular-cli/wiki/stories`.

JSON for storing application metadata

On the same line as dependency managers, JSON is also used to store metadata for software projects. How is metadata different from application configuration explained in the preceding section? This can be differentiated from the fact that the configuration is a set of customized settings that is required for the applications working. So configuration data can be said as a type of metadata or subset of the metadata. To understand it completely, let us dive in through various implementations of JSON as metadata.

Metadata in Angular 5

In Angular, metadata is used while processing a class for some specific functionality. The metadata configures the class so that it can be used as a component or services. The metadata is implemented via class decorators or property metadata. We will be learning about the class decorators as it suits our JSON essential context.

In the Angular (above version 2) application, the first thing to learn about is `NgModule`.

> An `NgModule` *is a class adorned with the* `@NgModule` *decorator function. It takes a metadata object and it tells Angular how to compile your code.*
>
> *– angular.io*

Each class can be accompanied with a single decorator. In case of `NgModule` the class is already defined in Angular core libraries. We need to use `NgModule` class 's decorator to identify all the components, providers (also called services), and modules created by a developer or imported from Angular core.

Consider the following code from `app.modules.ts`:

```
@NgModule({
    imports: [
        BrowserModule
```

```
    ],
    declarations: [
        AppComponent
    ],
    providers: [],
    bootstrap: [
        AppComponent
    ]
})
```

In the preceding code, the NgModule class is invoked like a function with a JavaScript object as a parameter. Note that this can only be possible if we prefixed the NgModule keyword with an annotation operator @, which is a syntactical declaration of decorator.

One more example that can be presented is the Component class from Angular Core. In the app.component.ts file, we have the following snippet:

```
@Component({
  selector: 'app-root',
  templateUrl: './app.component.html',
  styleUrls: ['./app.component.css']
})
export class AppComponent {
  title = 'app';
}
```

Here we have decorated the AppComponent class with the @Component decorator. This literally means we have our own custom class AppComponent attached to the @Component decorator. The component metadata is used to specify the following:

- The name of the selector component, which is used as an HTML tag to host the specified component
- The template that needs to be loaded adjacent to the selector tag
- Finally, the CSS or stylesheet file

Note that the metadata is not optional all the time and it can be mandatory too. In the preceding case, for the component class passing a selector and specifying a template is mandatory for Angular to load a component in UI.

This is how we implement the concept of JSON metadata in the Angular framework. Now let us move towards Node.js. We have already learned what is Node.js as technology and what is the package.json in the preceding section. Now let us learn about using constants JSON data across the Node.js application. We are going to create a sample Node.js server using constants in the next section.

Constants in Node.js

In Node.js, you can define your metadata as constants and use it in your application across the modules. To implement it consider the following snippet that is used to start a basic server in Node.js:

```
const http = require('http');
const constants = require('./constants');
const port = constants.port;
http.createServer((req, res) => {
    res.end(`Hello ${constants.audience}`);
}).listen(port);
console.log(`Node Server is running on port : ${port}`)
```

We have already studied node servers in the previous chapter. Just to describe in brief the code creates an HTTP server and listens for incoming requests on specified ports locally. Unlike that example, in the Chapter 6, *Building the Carousel Application*, we have imported a constants module.

The constants.js module contains the following code block:

```
module.exports = {
    "port" : 3300,
    "audience" : "readers"
}
```

The preceding code consists of an exported JSON. All the keys are constants and they work as singletons across other modules. Note that these keys are mutable only when a node process is loaded and doesn't perform a permanent write operation.

In Node.js, such constants files can contain any configurable data to start an application or the data that can be used globally across all modules. To be more specific, the port key is a configuration type metadata key and audience can be called a constant type metadata.

Template embedding

Embedding a template is the process of interpolating data models into the view. Here model can be a JSON or a simple string. The process of template embedding gave rise to new trending frontend technologies such as react.js, ember.js, handlebars.js, and so on. Using such template engines one can develop web clients in the Node.js server itself. This made JavaScript an isomorphic technology. Let us implement such mechanisms at our server side using handlerbar.js.

`handlebar.js` is a simple templating engine that is capable of embedding the JSON data into templates. When I say simple, I mean it. Let's check it out by implementing it in our node server by following these steps:

1. First, we need to install `handlebar` as a node module using the following command:

```
npm install --save handlebars
```

2. Once installation is complete, we can include the `handlebar` modules in our `app.js`:

```
const handlebar = require('handlebars');
```

3. Before working with `handlebar` modules, let us create an HTML that we need to send via response.
   The following `index.html.js` file contains template data:

```
module.exports = `
<!DOCTYPE html>
<html>
<head>
  <title>Hello readers</title>
</head>
<body>
  <h2>Greeting audience!</h2>
  <h3>Life is beautiful</h3>
</body>
</html>
```

The naming convention is followed (not standard though) with respect to taking into consideration HTML data, which is exported as node modules using the `js` extension.

4. Now we are going to create a route for HTML response as `/html`. The following are the modifications required to send HTML as a response:

```
const http = require('http');
const constants = require('./constants');
const template = require('./index.html');
const port = constants.port;
const handlebar = require('handlebars');
//console.log("template",);
http.createServer((req, res) => {

  if(req.url == '/html'){
```

```
        res.setHeader('content-type', 'text/html');
        res.end(template);
    }else
        res.end(`Hello ${constants.audience}`);
}).listen(port);
console.log(`Node Server is running on port : ${port}`)
```

In the preceding code, we imported the template file `require('./index.html')`. Next, we set the response headers as `text/html` so that our client browser gets an idea about how to interpret the received response from the server.

5. Furthermore, on requesting our node server with `http://localhost:3300/html`, we receive the following output:

6. Now let's embed the same template with different sets of data. To illustrate it, let's change the words `audience` to `readers` and the word `beautiful` to `simple`. To implement this we need two placeholders in our HTML, which can be done as follows:

```
//index.html.js
module.exports = `
<!DOCTYPE html>
<html>
<head>
    <title>Hello readers</title>
</head>
<body>
    <h2>Greeting {{audience}}!</h2>
    <h3>Life is {{adjective}}</h3>
</body>
</html>
```

7. Next, we need to create a model with keys `audience` and `adjective`:

```
{
    "audience": "Readers",
    "adjective": "simple"
}
```

8. Now to embed new data (JSON) we are going to update our code as follows:

```
const templateData = handlebar.compile(template)({
    "audience": "Readers",
    "adjective": "simple"
})
```

The `handlebar` has a `compile` method as a property. This method embeds the JSON data into HTML. Last but not least, let's not forget to change the response data from `template` to `templateData`:

```
res.end(templateData);
```

9. Restart the node server and hit the URL: `localhost:3300/html` to get the following output in the browser:

Note that the text `beautiful` is replaced by `simple`. This looks cool and we can say that an isomorphic app is ready! This was a simple prototype. We can add some complexity to template data by rendering it using arrays, objects, and so on, whenever required. The `handlebar` is a stable library and is capable of handling it. For more details about the `handlebar` library, check out this link: `http://handlebarsjs.com/`.

Comparisons with YAML

YAML is another software language-agnostic data interchange format that is slowly gaining popularity. YAML is a recursive acronym for YAML Ain't Markup Language, and it is commonly used to store metadata such as configurations, schemas, and properties. YAML is considered a human-readable data serialization standard and it depends on white spaces, positioning, and simple characters for line terminators, similar to popular scripting languages such as Ruby and Python. YAML is particular about the spacing between the elements and is not tab friendly. Similar to JSON, YAML key/value pairs are separated by a colon. Similar to text formatting, hyphens are used to indicate list items, unlike JSON where the list items are placed in an array or a child object. Since YAML is software language-agnostic, we would need parsers to understand the contents in that file. Such parsers are available for most of the popular languages such as PHP, Python, C++, Ruby, and JavaScript. Let's build the `config.json` file in YAML to understand what YAML is:

```
schema.json          x       config.yaml          x
1
2
3     PROJECT: "test project"
4     ENV: "DEV"
5     AUTOLOAD:
6        - "class1.php"
7        - "class2.php"
8        - "class3.php"
9     EXCLUDE:
10       - "project_x"
11       - "vendor"
12    RECURSIVE: "true"
13
```

Similar to our config JSON object, the YAML file contains all the data; the difference is in how the data is being arranged—as a list of items—and in how spacing and positioning are used to arrange lists of data. There are multiple YAML resources that are available on the internet to validate, serialize, and unserialize the YAML data.

For more information about YAML, please visit `http://www.yaml.org`, which is represented in YAML format.

Summary

JSON is quickly becoming the most popular data interchange format on the internet, but it is not limited to data exchange. In this chapter, we saw the usage of JSON to store metadata for dependency managers, package managers, configuration managers, and metadata stores. We were introduced to YAML, which is considered as an alternative to JSON. In the next chapter, we will look at the different resources that we can use to debug, validate, and format JSON.

8
Introduction to hapi.js

Over the last few years, the Node community has developed at a very fast rate. A variety of frameworks have evolved. Such frameworks are benchmarked with various aspects, such as code complexity, architecture patterns, performance, and also community usage. Some frameworks, such as Express and Koa, are known for their minimalist nature, and others, such as hapi and sails, provide configurable or structural coding techniques.

In this chapter, we are going to learn about `hapi.js` as it is a configuration-based framework. It uses JavaScript objects as configuration data, not always the pure JSON but the typical object notation provided as JavaScript literals. This chapter increments our learning curve toward the implementation and extensibility of JSON for creating a JavaScript server using hapi frameworks.

We are planning to study hapi with the help of the following guidelines:

- Basic server setup using JSON
- Configuring API using JSON
- Using JSON metadata and constants
- Testing hapi server APIs using POSTMAN
- JSON beneath POSTMAN

So, without any further ado, let's move on to our first section.

Basic server setup using JSON

In Chapter 7, *Alternate Implementations of JSON*, we already scaffolded a Node server while we worked on the *template embedding* section. We can either modify it or create a new app. If you are planning to use the same app, you need to do the following:

- Modify the `app.js`
- Eliminate template-related implementation

After modification, we get following structure in our code base:

```
EXPLORER                    JS app.js    ✕
▶ OPEN EDITORS              1   const http = require('http');
◢ UNTITLED (WO..            2   const constants = require('./constants');
                           3   const port = constants.port;
  ◢ test-node-app          4
    ▶ node_modules         5   http.createServer((req, res) => {
    JS app.js              6       res.end("Hello readers");
    JS constants.js        7   }).listen(port);
    {} package-lock.json   8   console.log(`Node Server is running on port : ${port}`)
    {} package.json        9
```

Just to get a brief idea about the preceding code, we created a simple HTTP server. The `createServer` method contains the request parameters `req` to handle the incoming request and the response instance for the outgoing response to and from the server respectively. We are using the `end` method of the response object to send response data as `Hello readers` to the client.

Let's go through proper stepwise procedure as shown as follows:

1. First let us install the `hapi` framework using the following command; we install a version greater than or equal to `v17.x.x`. By default, the package manager will install the latest for us; just make sure by verifying it in `package.json` after the installation is complete. Here is the installation command for the same:

   npm install hapi --save

Node package manager installs a new dependency called `hapi` in the node modules of our app.

2. Further, we need to include the `hapi` module in our `app.js`, which can be done as follows:

   ```
   const Hapi = require('hapi');
   ```

Including hapi modules enables us to leverage all the features of the hapi framework.

3. Now let us start by creating a basic `hapi` server. Here is the code!

```
const Hapi = require('hapi');
const constants = require('./constants');
const port = constants.port;
const server = new Hapi.Server({
    port
});
server.start();
console.log(`Server running at: ${server.info.uri}`);
```

In the preceding code, we did the following:

- We required a `hapi` module, just like any other node module.
- We already had a custom constants module that provided some configuration data. For now, we are only going to use port from constants.
- We created a new instance of the `hapi` server using the `server` method. Readers need to note that we are using JSON as configuration data for the server.
- Finally, we are using the `start` method of the server instance to initialize the server. The start method acts as a trigger to start a specific server.

Consider a scenario when a development team is planning to handle two server instances. With the same configuration, the initialization of the server can be conditionally switched easily. This can be visualized using the following pseudo-code:

```
If(server1 is configured)
    Server1.start()
else
    server2.start()
```

Or you can go parallel:

```
Server1.start();
Server2.start();
```

Both instances cannot run on the same port.

4. Now let us initialize our server by executing the command `node app.js`:

```
brunos-MacBook-Pro:test-node-app bruno$ node app.js
Server running at: http://brunos-MacBook-Pro.local:3300
```

The server starts running on `http://localhost:3300`.

In the preceding output, don't be confused with the profile name of the machine mentioned in the URL. This is because it serves as a localhost. If we put the preceding address in our browser, we will receive an error code notifying an error message `not found`. This is because we have not configured any API URL endpoints. We will work on that in the next section. Before learning about APIs, let's learn something more about configuring our startup command in `package.json`. This can be one more feature that can be noted by our readers under the topic of configuration using JSON.

Using JSON metadata and constants

We have already seen that using `node app.js` as a command boots our server and, yes, we know about that. But we have not learned to configure the command. **Node package manager (npm)** provides a way to configure our server `start` command using a `scripts` key in a `package.json`. This can be shown in the following snippet of `package.json`:

```
{
    "name": "test-node-app",
    "version": "1.0.0",
    "description": "",
    "main": "index.js",
    "scripts": {
      "test": "echo \"Error: no test specified\" &amp;amp;&amp;amp; exit
1",
      "start": "node app.js"
    },
    "author": "",
    "license": "ISC",
    "dependencies": {
        "handlebars": "^4.0.11",
        "hapi": "^17.2.0"
    }
}
```

In the preceding code, we added a `start` key inside the script's literals and provided our actual Node server start command as the value. Now let's run our new command as follows:

npm start

Woot! Our server starts running. Here the `start` key is already recognized by npm as the default command input to start the server. This is not the actually customized one. We can further customize it by naming it `new-start`. To do this, we need to make the following change in our `package.json`:

```
{
    "name": "test-node-app",
    "version": "1.0.0",
    "description": "",
    "main": "index.js",
    "scripts": {
        "test": "echo \"Error: no test specified\" &amp;amp;&amp;amp; exit
1",
        "start": "node app.js",
        "new-start": "node app.js"
    },
    "author": "",
    "license": "ISC",
    "dependencies": {
        "handlebars": "^4.0.11",
        "hapi": "^17.2.0"
    }
}
```

Now, to run our server with the customized startup command, we need to write it as follows:

npm run new-start

The npm parses the `package.json` and finds the `new-start` key and its corresponding command that needs to be executed. Such a startup feature is not specific to a framework such as `hapi.js`, but it is related to `package.json` which can be found in any npm frameworks. You can also use it for Express, Sails, Koa, or any other framework.

This is just the start for implementation of JSON for various scenarios. The `hapi` server is all about configuring the whole code base. Let's check in the next section how can the routes can be configured using JavaScript object notation.

Configuring API using JSON

What is an **API**? To put it simply, an **application programming interface** is a way in which we can access our application data and present it in a desired format. The API implementation grants access to its data via application requests. It can be an HTTP request or FTP. With respect to the context of our book, we are going to learn about HTTP requests.

A request basically consists of the following:

- **Unique Resource Location** (URL)
- Request headers
- Request body

An API server provides an endpoint URL so that we can access the required info through our client, for instance, a browser. In the preceding chapters, we have already seen how node.js implements an API server with its basic core.

Let's see how `hapi` implements such an API on top of node.js. To discover this, consider the following code:

```
const Hapi = require('hapi');
const constants = require('./constants');
const port = constants.port;

const server = new Hapi.Server({
 port
});

server.route({
  method: 'GET',
  path:'/greetings',
  handler(request, h) {
      return 'hello readers!';
  }
});
server.start();
console.log(`Server running at: ${server.info.uri}`);
```

Before finding out about the code, let's check the output in the browser by hitting the URL as follows: `http://localhost:3300/greetings`.

We receive the output as **Hello readers!**

In the preceding snippet, we have introduced a new method called `route` of a `hapi` server instance. The minimum configuration required for the route to function is provided with three keys: method, path and handler. They are explained as follows:

- **Method**: This is an HTTP resource method that is required to access the resource on the HTTP server. The other basic methods can be `GET`, `POST`, `PUT`, and `DELETE`. In our case, we are using the `GET` method, hence it is specified so.

- **Path**: The path is nothing but a URL or an endpoint. Such endpoints work concatenated with domains to locate and request the specific data from any client, such as a browser. In our case, we are using `http://localhost:3300/greetings`.

- **Handler**: Each URL path has a specific aim or provides some kind of functionality adjoining its method. Such functionality is yielded using a handler function. The handler key has a callback function with two parameters as per Hapi v17.2.0:

  - The first parameter is an instance request received. The request instance consists of all the requested information, such as requested headers, URL parameters, body, events, raw node request instance, and so on.

  - The second one is a combination of the `hapi` server instance plus context of the route configuration data that we provided.

The data returns in a `handler` callback that can be a simple string or complex JSON converted by `hapi` into a server response or even an HTML. The setting headers of such data types, such as content-type are handled by `hapi` itself.

Let us segregate the route functionality into a route-specific file. This can be done by the following step-wise procedure so that nothing is missed out:

1. Export the route configuration object from a separate file, let's call it `routes.js`, as follows:

```
//routes.js
module.exports = [{
  method: 'GET',
  path:'/greetings',
  handler(request, h) {
      return `<b>hello readers!</b>`;
  }
}]
```

Note that we have exported an array so that we can pass multiple route configuration objects in a single array.

2. Remove the route configuration object that existed in `app.js` and include the `routes.js` inside the `app.js` file:

```
const Hapi = require('hapi');
const constants = require('./constants');
const routes = require('./routes');
const port = constants.port;
const server = new Hapi.Server({
 port
});
server.route(routes);
server.start();
console.log(`Server running at: ${server.info.uri}`);
```

Note that we have passed the `routes` constant as a parameter to our `server.route` method. Restart the hapi server in the Terminal and you will receive the output. Segregating routes from an app is a good practice as it enhances the maintainability of our route controllers and keeps our `app.js` as simple as possible.

3. Restart the `hapi` server and verify whether everything is working fine by hitting the URL `http://localhost:3300/greetings` from the browser.

Configuring a plugin in hapi

Plugins provide a way to handle a business logic in a different piece of code. The implementation of the plugin can differ from middleware to any third-party utility methods used for a specific purpose.

Let's create a custom plugin to know how plugins work. To integrate plugins, we need to create a file called `plugins.js` in our application. The `plugin.js` consist of a snippet, which is presented as follows:

```
exports.logRequest = {
  register(server, options){
      console.log("A plugin got called!");
  },
  name : "logRequest"
}
```

The preceding code only contains the minimal properties required to compose a plugin.

The composition consists of a simple object with the `register` method and `name` as keys.

`register`: This is a callback method invoked explicitly when the plugin is attached for registration for a server in `app.js`. It is called during server initialization and not while on request event. Hence we moved the `server.start` method inside a `'then-able'` callback so that our server would wait until all plugins are loaded; to put it simply, handling the asynchronosity using built-in `Promise` library methods. All the modifications refer to the `app.js` file, which is presented as follows:

```
const Hapi = require('hapi');
const constants = require('./constants');
const routes = require('./routes');
const plugins = require('./plugins');
const port = constants.port;
const server = new Hapi.Server({ port });

server.route(routes);
server.register(plugins.logRequest)
.then(() => {
    server.start();
})
.catch((err) => {
    console.log("error", err);
})

console.log(`Server running at: ${server.info.uri}`);
```

As we are using `Promises` to handle the asynchronosity of plugins, when any error is thrown, the `catch` method handles it.

`name`: The plugins are defined with a `name` property for identification by `hapi`. Every custom plugin is named before it is used and it's a *mandatory* property.

Once you compose your plugin in the `hapi` server, run the code by restarting the `hapi` server and requesting via a browser with the URL `http://localhost:3300/greetings`.

Check the Terminal to get the following output:

```
A plugin got called!
Server running at: http://brunos-MacBook-Pro.local:3300
```

As per the hapi v17 release documentation, we have the following properties that can be used while implementing a plugin:

```
{ register, name, version, multiple, dependencies, once, pkg }
```

Moving toward some more advanced learning, let's build a plugin to log the URL in the console of the Terminal every time a request is received. Here is a step-wise procedure to get it through:

1. Listen to the `onRequest` event in the plugin using the server instance of the register method. node.js is implemented using an event-driven model as its backbone. The `onRequest` is triggered when a request is received by a server at its runtime. This can be done as follows:

    ```
    server.ext('onRequest', (request, reply)=>{
        console.log("Listening to request!");
    })
    ```

2. By now, if you have restarted your server and hit the greetings URL, you may have received an error; the error is because we have not instructed our event loop what to do next. To handle the request and pass it on to the controller methods, we need to use `return` with `reply.continue`:

    ```
    server.ext('onRequest', (request, reply)=>{
        console.log("Listening to request!");
        return reply.continue;
    })
    ```

The `continue` property is implemented as a property of the reply instance but consists of data which is a symbol data type as per new ecmascript. If we console the reply instance, we can find a couple of properties, such as `close`, `abandon`, and so on, that can instruct the event loop to do the needful.

3. We have successfully implemented a mechanism to handle all the requests by now. Last but not least, we need to extract the URL from the request instance. Let us do this as shown below and sum up all the code:

    ```
    //plugin.js
    exports.logRequest = {
      register(server, options){
          console.log("A plugin got called!");
          server.ext('onRequest', (request, reply)=>{
              console.log("Listening to request!");
              const path = request.url.path;
              const target = request.url.query.target;
    ```

```
            console.log(`The target is ${target} for url : ${path}`);
            return reply.continue;
        })
    },
    name : "logRequest"
}
```

We can print the request instance in the console to find all the properties that it provides. For now, we are using the URL property which provides all the requested URL data, such as the URL path and query parameters that can be passed via the URL. We will be using a `target` key as the query parameter in the `/greetings` URL. The URL form is as follows: `http://localhost:3300/greetings?target=developers`.

Let us restart our server using `npm start` to get the following output:

```
> node app.js

A plugin got called!
Server running at: http://brunos-MacBook-Pro.local:3300
Listening to request!
The target is undefined for url : /greetings
Listening to request!
The target is undefined for url : /favicon.ico
```

The composition of such a plugin using JavaScript objects yields incremental app development and modularization of code. This results in the maintainability of code for long project work.

Testing the APIs using POSTMAN

The API endpoint we created (`http://localhost:3300/greetings`) is a GET method request type API call and it is quite easy to test the API endpoint directly in the browser URL locator. This is because when you hit any URL input from the browser URL locator directly, by default it performs a GET method request. So what about the POST, PUT, or DELETE request methods? Definitely, the browser is able to make those requests but not by default or through any direct input in the URL locator but by using AJAX requests or FORM POST requests.

In such cases, if we have created an API server and now we want to test our URL endpoint for sanity with respect to other request methods, we can't do it directly. Either we need to write some JavaScript code at the client side to make those API calls or use a REST client such as POSTMAN that can make API calls for us.

Testing hapi server APIs using POSTMAN

Let us install POSTMAN for our use case of the `hapi` server APIs and test it. Simply do the following:

1. Follow the URL `https://www.getpostman.com/`
2. Download this app according to your operating system and install it

The following screenshot shows a view of the *POSTMAN* app:

Now we just need to enter the required details for making an HTTP request from this client. Let us go step-wise so that we don't miss anything:

1. Enter the URL through which we want to request our data. In our case, we have `http://localhost:3300/greetings`.

2. Preceding the request URL input is the request method selection drop-down menu. Check whether the intended request method is selected. The `GET` method is selected by default or else we can opt for others whenever required.

3. Check whether any URL or header parameters are required to be sent. In our case, we have a URL parameter as `target`. The following screenshot shows the overall data:

Click on the **Send** button to receive the request data. This is how we can test and debug each and every API while developing it. The benefit it offers is reduces the debugging time and also on-demand execution of asynchronous requests whenever desired.

JSON beneath POSTMAN

The *POSTMAN* app is intended to provide more than actually what we saw, which was just one important feature. We can integrate all the API endpoints into one collection and run them together.

We can also intercept POSTMAN client with the browser's POSTMAN interceptor extension. This helps us to view our browser request directly in the *POSTMAN* app without manual interaction. We can even export the collections of endpoints for portability purposes.

Such amazing features are of great use during any API server development. If you visit POSTMAN LABS (`https://github.com/postmanlabs`), where all the POSTMAN repositories are open sourced and provided for the community, you will find out how extensive JSON is used extensively, especially in its POSTMAN collection repo: `https://github.com/postmanlabs/postman-collection`.

Let us study the collection feature using the following step-wise procedure so that we are able to gain insights into how JSON is used beneath the app:

1. At the right side of the app, we have two sections: **History** and **Collection**. Previously, when we made an API call, the call was recorded in the **History** section of the app. Let us navigate to the **History** section and click on the options (indicated with three dots) as shown in the following screenshot:

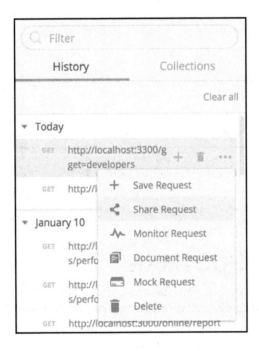

Select the **Save Request** option from the popup; you will get a **SAVE REQUEST** dialog box.

2. You can keep same request URL as the name or change it to something like `Greeting url`. Further, we need to create a collection into which we can save our request. This can be done in same dialog box as follows:

Click on the **Save** button to save the request data into the selected collection.

3. Once the collection is saved, go to the collection's options and select **Export** from the popup. Select the required options and export the data. A JSON file is stored on your machine. If we view that file in any of sublime, we get the following data:

```json
{

    "variables": [],
    "info":
    {
        "name": "node-test-app",
        "_postman_id": "5f507e82-d39d-e96e-edc5-efa2fd3c11b1",
        "description": "",
        "schema":
"https://schema.getpostman.com/json/collection/v2.0.0/collection.json"
    },
    "item": [
        {
            "name": "Greetings url",
            "request":
            {
                "url":
                {
"raw": "http://localhost:3300/greetings?target=developers",
                    "protocol": "http",
                    "host": [
                        "localhost"
                    ],
                    "port": "3300",
                    "path": [
                        "greetings"
                    ],
                    "query": [
                        {
                            "key": "target",
                            "value": "developers",
                            "equals": true,
                            "description": ""
                        }
                    ],
                    "variable": []
                },
                "method": "GET",
                "header": [],
                "body":
```

```
                {},
                "description": ""
            },
            "response": []
        }
    ]
}
```

All the data is in the form of pure JSON. Therefore, we can say that POSTMAN maintains the data in the form of JSON. Such a format provides easy readability and data portability within applications as well.

 The code base can be referred the git repo link: `https://github.com/bron10/json-essentials-book/tree/master/chapter%209`.

Summary

The configurable server using a JavaScript object is truly fascinating and so speedy to work with. Maybe, at the start, it takes little time to set up the whole configurable objects but once sorted, it provides great flexibility to reuse the snippets as well as maintaining the code. It seems like the `hapi` server is prepared for scalability from the start. Moreover, as we saw, we don't need to handle all the data response from the server or its content, just return the data to the callback handler and `hapi` identifies its type by itself. The development time to define content-type or find an `npm` package for each response type, such as HTML, JSON, or any string, is reduced to a great extent.

Lastly, we saw the debugging process using the POSTMAN client and its usage. Creating a whole hapi server system makes extensive use of JSON itself and it is one of the important learning steps for us in the application of JSON at the server side. Moving on to the next chapter, we are going to explore a NoSQL database known as MongoDB and even integrate our app with it for persistence storage.

Storing JSON Documents in MongoDB

9

NoSQL databases are emerging as the next big thing. From the field of geospatial data to small businesses, the implementation of NoSQL databases has increased exponentially. This is due to the flexibility they provide while managing data, which we are going to study in detail in this chapter.

A NoSQL database is something that doesn't adhere to relational databases, that is, databases that are not structured, unlike tabular format. Such NoSQL databases can accommodate a variety of data models, such as graphs, single-level or multilevel key-value pairs, or simply JSON documents, and so on. MongoDB is a type of NoSQL database that uses BSON document storage. Let's dive into this topic by learning about the following points:

- Setting up MongoDB and integrating with the hapi app
- JSON versus BSON
- Inserting a JSON document
- Retrieving a JSON document
- JSON-based schemas in MongoDB

Setting up MongoDB

Installing MongoDB on the system is quite simple for operating systems such as Linux, macOS, and versions above Windows 7. The Windows 7 version requires some patch installation. We are not going to focus on each and every installation step on every operating system, as that will take us out of context. We are planning for minimal installation steps and focusing mainly on our goals of this chapter. Therefore, we are going to install MongoDB on macOS using Homebrew:

> For readers who are Windows users, follow this link for more information: `https://docs.mongodb.com/tutorials/install-mongodb-on-windows/`.
>
> Or for Linux users, here is the link: `https://docs.mongodb.com/manual/tutorial/install-mongodb-on-linux/`.
>
> For macOS users, follow this link: `https://docs.mongodb.com/manual/tutorial/install-mongodb-on-os-x/`.

Homebrew is a package manager for macOS.

Make sure you install Homebrew (`https://brew.sh/`) first so that the `brew` command is available. Here is the procedure for setting up MongoDB that we need to follow:

1. Install the `mongodb` package using the following command: `brew install mongodb`.
2. Once the installation is complete, before running the mongoDB service, we need to assign permission to `/data/db` directories. These directories are configured to save the mongoDB databases. As the data directory is created at the root level, we need to provide permission of for the mongoDB application user to access the directory. This can be done with the following command:

```
sudo chown -R `id -un` /data/db
```

We are setting access to all the directories inside the `data` directory recursively. It is recommended to use the `chown` command rather than the `chmod` command, which may grant access to the other users too.

3. Run `mongod` inside the Terminal; we will receive the log that provides details regarding connection with `mongodb` and its storage engine **WiredTiger**.

4. After installation and once the data directory is configured successfully, we need to check whether `mongodb` runs well on our system. This can be done by running the following command:

mongod

The `mongod` service is executed on running the preceding command. We get the following log:

```
Last login: Tue Jan 23 11:05:10 on ttys008
brunos-MacBook-Pro:~ bruno$ mongod
2018-01-30T11:12:53.470+0530 I CONTROL  [initandlisten] MongoDB starting : pid=13488 port=27017 dbpath=/data/db 64-bit host=brunos-MacBook-Pro.local
2018-01-30T11:12:53.470+0530 I CONTROL  [initandlisten] db version v3.6.2
2018-01-30T11:12:53.470+0530 I CONTROL  [initandlisten] git version: 489d177dbd0f0420a8ca04d39fd78d0a2c539420
2018-01-30T11:12:53.470+0530 I CONTROL  [initandlisten] OpenSSL version: OpenSSL 1.0.2n  7 Dec 2017
2018-01-30T11:12:53.470+0530 I CONTROL  [initandlisten] allocator: system
2018-01-30T11:12:53.470+0530 I CONTROL  [initandlisten] modules: none
2018-01-30T11:12:53.470+0530 I CONTROL  [initandlisten] build environment:
2018-01-30T11:12:53.470+0530 I CONTROL  [initandlisten]     distarch: x86_64
2018-01-30T11:12:53.470+0530 I CONTROL  [initandlisten]     target_arch: x86_64
2018-01-30T11:12:53.470+0530 I CONTROL  [initandlisten] options: {}
2018-01-30T11:12:53.470+0530 I -        [initandlisten] Detected data files in /data/db created by the 'wiredTiger' storage engine, so setting the active storage engine to 'wiredTiger'.
2018-01-30T11:12:53.471+0530 I STORAGE  [initandlisten] wiredtiger_open config: create,cache_size=3584M,session_max=20000,eviction=(threads_min=4,threads_max=4),config_base=false,statistics=(fast),log=(enabled=true,archive=true,path=journal,compressor=snappy),file_manager=(close_idle_time=100000),statistics_log=(wait=0),verbose=(recovery_progress),
2018-01-30T11:12:53.692+0530 I STORAGE  [initandlisten] WiredTiger message [1517290973:692842][13488:0x7fff892b9340], txn-recover: Main recovery loop: starting at 13/768
2018-01-30T11:12:53.804+0530 I STORAGE  [initandlisten] WiredTiger message [1517290973:804444][13488:0x7fff892b9340], txn-recover: Recovering log 13 through 14
2018-01-30T11:12:53.887+0530 I STORAGE  [initandlisten] WiredTiger message [1517290973:887801][13488:0x7fff892b9340], txn-recover: Recovering log 14 through 14
2018-01-30T11:12:54.096+0530 I CONTROL  [initandlisten]
2018-01-30T11:12:54.096+0530 I CONTROL  [initandlisten] ** WARNING: Access control is not enabled for the database.
2018-01-30T11:12:54.096+0530 I CONTROL  [initandlisten] **          Read and write access to data and configuration is unrestricted.
2018-01-30T11:12:54.096+0530 I CONTROL  [initandlisten]
2018-01-30T11:12:54.096+0530 I CONTROL  [initandlisten] ** WARNING: This server is bound to localhost.
2018-01-30T11:12:54.096+0530 I CONTROL  [initandlisten] **          Remote systems will be unable to connect to this server.
2018-01-30T11:12:54.096+0530 I CONTROL  [initandlisten] **          Start the server with --bind_ip <address> to specify which IP
2018-01-30T11:12:54.096+0530 I CONTROL  [initandlisten] **          addresses it should serve responses from, or with --bind_ip_all to
2018-01-30T11:12:54.096+0530 I CONTROL  [initandlisten] **          bind to all interfaces. If this behavior is desired, start the
2018-01-30T11:12:54.096+0530 I CONTROL  [initandlisten] **          server with --bind_ip 127.0.0.1 to disable this warning.
2018-01-30T11:12:54.096+0530 I CONTROL  [initandlisten]
2018-01-30T11:12:54.103+0530 I FTDC     [initandlisten] Initializing full-time diagnostic data capture with directory '/data/db/diagnostic.data'
2018-01-30T11:12:54.104+0530 I NETWORK  [initandlisten] waiting for connections on port 27017
```

In the preceding screenshot, our `mongodb` is waiting for incoming requests on a default port 27017. One more thing that to be noticed in above screenshot is the term WiredTiger. WiredTiger is an efficient storage engine acquired by mongodb for high scalability of apps on the mongo database system and is integrated with mongodb from version 3.2 . The preceding screenshot also provides the current version of mongodb, which is `db version v3.6.2`.

Once we complete the setup with mongodb, in the next section we are going to connect our *hapi* app with mongodb for persistence storage.

Connecting the hapi app with MongoDB

Once the installation is complete, we are ready to rock with MongoDB. In Chapter 8, *Introduction to hapi.js*, we had our hapi server scaffolded. We going to use the same structure to learn about MongoDB.

To leverage all the features of the MongoDB, it provides a client mongoDB node module through npm. We need to install the mongodb client in our node-test-app directory which was created previously. We can directly get the code base from GitHub at https://github.com/bron10/json-essentials-book.

We need to run the following command in the Terminal:

```
npm install mongodb --save
```

The preceding command will install a mongodb client in node modules of our hapi server app and will register itself in package.json as follows:

```
{
    "name": "test-node-app",
    "version": "1.0.0",
    "description": "",
    "main": "index.js",
    "scripts": {
        "test": "echo \"Error: no test specified\" && exit 1",
        "start": "node app.js",
        "new-start": "node app.js"
    },
    "author": "",
    "license": "ISC",
    "dependencies": {
        "handlebars": "^4.0.11",
        "hapi": "^17.2.0",
        "mongodb": "^3.0.2"
    }
}
```

Once we have the mongodb package in our node module, we are ready to use it in our code. We need to require mongodb and configure it with connection credentials as follows:

```
const Hapi = require('hapi');
const constants = require('./constants');
const routes = require('./routes');
const plugins = require('./plugins');
const port = constants.port;
const server = new Hapi.Server({ port });
const MongoClient = require('mongodb').MongoClient;
MongoClient.connect(constants.mongodb.url, function(err, client) {
    if (err)
        throw err;
    console.log("Connected successfully to mongodb server");
});
server.route(routes);
server.register(plugins.logRequest)
    .then(() => {
        server.start();
    })
    .catch((err) => {
        console.log("error", err);
    })
console.log(`Server running at: ${server.info.uri}`);
```

Let's understand the code step by step as follows:

1. Including `require('mongodb')`. MongoClient provides a `mongo` instance which in return provides a prototype method called `connect`, which is responsible for establishing a connection with the mongoDB client.

2. The `connect` method accepts the `mongo` server URL. Note a JSON-based solution here that is implemented as a configuration provider called `constant.js`. We use the `constants.mongodb.url` address to access the URL data from constant JSON. The URL placed in `constant.js` comprises the IP address (used as localhost) and default port `27017`. This is as follows:

```
//constants.js
module.exports = {
    "port": 3300,
    "audience": "readers",
    "mongodb": {
        "url": "mongodb://localhost:27017"
    }
}
```

3. The second parameter of `MongoClient.connect` is a callback function which is invoked once the `mongo` client tries to establish a connection to MongoDB. As this code is synchronous, we are using a callback. The resultant error or success during connection establishment is handled in the callback.

On booting our server using `npm start`, we get the following output:

```
Server running at: http://brunos-MacBook-Pro.local:3300
Connected successfully to mongodb server
```

Now, to handle the asynchronous code in a more effective way, we are going to implement promises. We have already learned about `Promises` in Chapter 3, *AJAX Requests with JSON*. Just to recap, a `Promise` is boilerplate code to handle asynchronous success or error data more effectively than a normal callback. It provides a better code structure and maintains code readability. We are going to continue with our code by promisifying the mongoDB client, which looks as follows:

```
MongoClient.connect(constants.mongodb.url)
    .then(function() {
        console.log("Connected successfully to mongodb server")
    })
    .catch(function(err) {
        console.log("An error occurred while connecting to mongodb!", err)
    })
```

Note that we have established the connection with mongoDB on app initialization. Not closing the mongoDB connection is not a recommended way as it is prone to memory leak. Hence we need to do the following measures:

1. Move the mongodb connection method to `routes.js` and connect on every request
2. Close the connection once we complete our mongodb connection usage on every request

We are going to implement it while performing operations on the document. But first we need to know what collections and documents are in terms of MongoDB. Let's study this in the following sections.

JSON versus BSON

By now, we know JSON very well. Let's learn about BSON with three simple points:

- MongoDB drivers convert the incoming JSON to binary-encoded JSON called BSON and pass it to the storage engine, currently WiredTiger. Let us visualize it as follows:

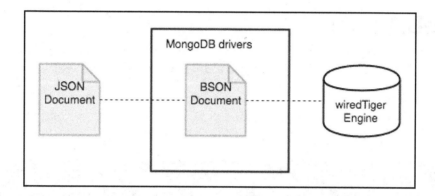

In the preceding diagram, the incoming JSON is converted to a binary-serialized JSON-like entity called a **BSON Document** and then stored in DB.

- The specifications of BSON provide various benefits, such as it has a small memory print as compared to JSON, it is traversable, and it can be queried as well as quickly parsed for any other language support
- When the BSON document is retrieved, the data types in BSON specs are converted to type native language data type by mongoDB drivers, which are in turn used by the developer

The developer has nothing to do with BSON directly, they will be working with JSON. It is the MongoDB driver that handles everything.

 For more info on BSON, you can follow this link: `http://bsonspec.org/`.

Collections

As we store records or tuples in tables of the Structure Query Language, BSON documents are stored in collections of mongoDB in our case. A collection is single group of one or more BSON documents. It is a reference that points to the cluster of documents together. We will be demonstrating the view of the documents in the following section.

MongoDB shell

The MongoDB provides built-in shell or Terminal access to the databases and performs raw operations. Let's insert simple JSON data into a collection called `customers`.

Assuming our `mongod` service is already running on the system, open a new Terminal. Type the command `mongo` to open a new mongo shell followed by one more command, called `show dbs`. This will provide the following view in the Terminal:

```
Last login: Fri Feb  2 09:23:10 on ttys007
brunos-MacBook-Pro:~ bruno$ mongo
MongoDB shell version v3.6.2
connecting to: mongodb://127.0.0.1:27017
MongoDB server version: 3.6.2
Server has startup warnings:
2018-02-02T09:33:41.797+0530 I CONTROL  [initandlisten]
2018-02-02T09:33:41.797+0530 I CONTROL  [initandlisten] ** WARNING: Access control is not enabled for the database.
2018-02-02T09:33:41.797+0530 I CONTROL  [initandlisten] **          Read and write access to data and configuration is unrestricted.
2018-02-02T09:33:41.797+0530 I CONTROL  [initandlisten]
2018-02-02T09:33:41.797+0530 I CONTROL  [initandlisten] ** WARNING: This server is bound to localhost.
2018-02-02T09:33:41.797+0530 I CONTROL  [initandlisten] **          Remote systems will be unable to connect to this server.
2018-02-02T09:33:41.797+0530 I CONTROL  [initandlisten] **          Start the server with --bind_ip <address> to specify which IP
2018-02-02T09:33:41.797+0530 I CONTROL  [initandlisten] **          addresses it should serve responses from, or with --bind_ip_all to
2018-02-02T09:33:41.797+0530 I CONTROL  [initandlisten] **          bind to all interfaces. If this behavior is desired, start the
2018-02-02T09:33:41.797+0530 I CONTROL  [initandlisten] **          server with --bind_ip 127.0.0.1 to disable this warning.
2018-02-02T09:33:41.797+0530 I CONTROL  [initandlisten]
2018-02-02T09:33:41.797+0530 I CONTROL  [initandlisten]
2018-02-02T09:33:41.797+0530 I CONTROL  [initandlisten] ** WARNING: soft rlimits too low. Number of files is 256, should be at least 1000
> show dbs
admin       0.000GB
local       0.000GB
restaurants 0.000GB
test        0.000GB
> use test
switched to db test
>
```

`show dbs` provides the list of the databases present in the mongoDB 's /data/db directory we configured previously.

We can note one more command, called `use test`. `use` is a powerful command that either creates a new database and selects it for usage or just selects the already existing ones. In the preceding case, we have used databases that already existed.

Once we select a DB, we need to create a collection. In mongodb, we don't have to maintain any schema. It is up to the developer or administrator to structure a collection as per requirement. Such flexibility is amazing as the structure can be developed at development time itself, thus reducing the database design time.

Previously, we defined a collection as a reference to document, nothing else. So until we have any JSON document (BSON) inserted into our collection, a collection is of no use or it may not exist in that case. Let us create a collection called `customer` by inserting a new JSON document as shown in the following code:

```
db.customers.insert({
    "cust_id": 1,
    "firstname": "John",
    "lastname": "Doe",
    "Address": {
        "pincode": "909001",
        "street": "3305 Tenmile",
        "city": "LA"
    }
})
```

In the preceding snippet, we are inserting a JSON document consisting of customer information such as name and address inside the collection `customer`. Run this snippet inside the shell as a command.

We can retrieve all the data by using the `find` method from the collection instance `db.customers`. The snippet to retrieve the data is as follows:

```
db.customers.find().pretty()
```

We can sum up the overall operations that we performed on our collection in the following screenshot:

```
> db.customers.insert({"cust_id":1,"firstname":"John","lastname":"Doe","Address":{"pincode":"900001","street":"3305 Tenmile","city":"LA"}})
WriteResult({ "nInserted" : 1 })
> db.customers.insert({
...     "cust_id": 2,
...     "firstname": "smith",
...     "lastname": "Tiger",
...     "Address":
...     {
...         "pincode": "900002",
...         "street": "3305 Twentymile",
...         "city": "LA"
...     }
... })
WriteResult({ "nInserted" : 1 })
>
> db.customers.find().pretty()
{
        "_id" : ObjectId("5a73e93236b515b8decde684"),
        "cust_id" : 1,
        "firstname" : "John",
        "lastname" : "Doe",
        "Address" : {
                "pincode" : "900001",
                "street" : "3305 Tenmile",
                "city" : "LA"
        }
}
{
        "_id" : ObjectId("5a73eb2436b515b8decde685"),
        "cust_id" : 2,
        "firstname" : "smith",
        "lastname" : "Tiger",
        "Address" : {
                "pincode" : "900002",
                "street" : "3305 Twentymile",
                "city" : "LA"
        }
}
>
```

In the mongo shell, the db is a reference variable used to refer to the collections. The collections provide the public methods, such as insert, find, drop, and so on. This is how the JSON data was managed via the mongo shell; let's use the mongo client module in the code so that we can access the collection documents programmatically.

Inserting a JSON document

The NoSQL writes are speedy as compared to the SQL write operation. This is because you don't have to maintain any schema from the start and its relevant data types.

Let us continue with our test-node-app and implement a POST API call that sets the customer's data in the collection.

The stepwise procedure is as follows:

1. By now, we have the mongoDb connection instance inside the `app.js` file. So first we need to remove the following code from `app.js`. Keep the code in some temp file as we are going to use it later:

```
const MongoClient = require('mongodb').MongoClient;
MongoClient.connect(constants.mongodb.url)
    .then(function() {
        console.log("Connected successfully to mongodb server")
    })
    .catch(function(err) {
    console.log("An error occurred while connecting to mongodb!", err)
    })
```

2. We are going to create a new piece of middleware that will use the existing DB connection to make a query to the particular collection. So go to `plugin.js` and add the following code to it:

```
exports.mongoConnect = {
    register(server, options){
        return MongoClient.connect(constants.mongodb.url)
        .then(function(client){
            console.log("Connected successfully to mongodb server");
            server.ext('onRequest', (request, reply)=>{
                    request.dbInstance = client.db('test');
                    return reply.continue;
            })
             return;
        })
        .catch(function(err){
        console.log("An error occurred while connecting to mongodb!",
err)
        return
        })
    },
    name : "mongoConnect"
}
```

In the preceding code, on successful establishment of a connection, we save the database instance on request event and inside the request singleton instance which is shared throughout the app.

Saving the db instance in `request.dbInstance` provides a way to pass and use the same instance throughout our request life cycle. We are going use this db instance in our handler created in the next step.

3. Now we are going to use the db instance to query the collection test via a new API handler. This will be a POST call made for the `http://localhost:3300/customer/add` URL. Here is the configurable object code that will be inserted into the file `routes.js`:

```
{
    method: 'POST',
    path: '/customer/add',
    handler(request, h){
        const dbInstance = request.dbInstance;
        const requestBody = request.payload;
        return dbInstance.collection('customer')
        .insert(requestBody)
            .then((insertedStatus) =>{
                return "customer added successfully";
            })
            .catch((err) =>{
                return new Error(err);
            })
    }
}
```

Using the collection instance of `customer`, we used the insert method that stored the request data from the payload.

4. Prepare the request data in POSTMAN or any other REST client. The following is an illustration of the request data format:

```
{
    "firstname": "Bron",
    "lastname": "Dave",
    "Address": {
        "pincode": 123456,
        "street": "Thirtymile",
        "city": "LC"
    }
}
```

Hit the API endpoint from either the REST client app or the browser extension called `postman` to get the following response:

Make sure the response status code received is `200` with the success message and the operation is said to be complete.

Retrieving a JSON document

We can perform the retrieval operation using the find method on a selected collection. Let us perform this operation by continuing with the add customers functionality and providing a list of already added customers on successful response. So, to demonstrate it, consider the following code:

```
{
    method: 'POST',
    path: '/customer/add',
    handler(request, h){
        const dbInstance = request.dbInstance;
```

```
const requestBody = request.payload;
const customerCollection = dbInstance.collection('customer');
return customerCollection.insert(requestBody)
    .then((insertedStatus) =>{
        return customerCollection.find(
            {})
            .toArray()
            .then((customerList) =>{
                return {
                    message: "customer added successfully",
                    customerList
                }
            })
    })
    .catch((err) =>{
        return new Error(err);
    })
}
}
```

Let's study the code carefully by going through the following points:

- The method `find`, when provided with an empty object as parameter, returns all the occurrences of selection; in our case, the customer's information
- We have used the `cursor.toArray` method to convert the resultant pointer data into specifically an array

There are various cursor methods. Follow this link for more details: `https://docs.mongodb.com/manual/reference/method/js-cursor/`.

But wait, what exactly is a cursor? A cursor is a pointer to the results or a reference. The find method returns such a reference to the results and on executing cursor methods, we extract the data from it.

- Lastly, we returned an object of success that comprises our success message and the `customerList` data.

The following screenshot sums everything up:

JSON-based schemas in MongoDB

There is a possibility that we may need the database's schema before the application development gets started. Or what if we want to set the data types for all the datasets with all kind of validations just like MySQL?

At this point, we are planning to structure and validate our NoSQL data. We are moving toward finding a framework that provides a wrapper around mongodb and which can yield such features with trusted community support.

Mongoose is a leading third-party framework that provides all kind of schema-based validations, virtual properties, and more.

Let us go through an approach for how JSON-based schemas are prepared and validated using `mongoose`:

1. Install mongoose via the following `npm` command: `npm install mongoose --save`

2. As we are planning to implement mongoose in our application, we are going to use the wrapper methods provided by mongoose to connect to mongoDB

Not a big modification, simply comment the mongodb client from `plugins.js` and include the following:

```
const MongoClient = require('mongoose');
```

This will assign the mongoose module methods in the `MongoClient` constant. Another minor change is there is no need to set `dbInstance` on request; mongoose does all the hard work for us. So let us comment out the `server.ext` event listener:

```
/**
server.ext('onRequest', (request, reply)=>{
    request.dbInstance = client.db('test');
    return reply.continue;
})**/
```

3. In mongoose, schemas are something that provide a blueprint of a mongodb model. They act as a structures that hold the incoming collection data in terms of consistency. So let's create a simple schema for our customer database in a new file, `model.js`:

```
const mongoose = require('mongoose');
module.exports.customers = mongoose.model('customers', {
"firstname": String,
"lastname": String,
"Address": { type: mongoose.Schema.ObjectId, ref: 'customers_address'
}
    });

    const Address = mongoose.model('customers_address', {
        "pincode": Number,
        "street": String,
        "city": String
    });
```

In the preceding snippet, we created a `customers` model which is specific to our `customer` collection. To speak in terms of RDBMS, we created a customers schema for the customers table. We can populate the keys, such as an address, with a collection of data type properties such as type, ref, default, and so on, or simply define the data type, such as the key `firstname` in the preceding snippet.

An important thing to focus on here is we have a reference type called `Address`. Mongoose enables us to nest the schema by using either the arrays or references data type. In the preceding case, we have used the type reference.

Next, the data type assign to each and every key, is just the way to define it but not the way to perform the actual validation. So if we send `pincode` as a string, it will get saved. But if we send defined `pincode` as a Boolean and request a string in payload for `pincode`, it will throw a type casting error. To validate the `pincode`, we can add a simple validator to our `customer_address` model as follows:

```
module.exports.customers_address = mongoose.model('customers_address', {
    "pincode": {
        type: Number,
        validate: {
            validator: function(v) {
                return `${v}`.length === 6;
            },
            message: '{VALUE} is not a valid pincode!'
        }
    },
    "street": String,
    "city": String
});
```

One of the most used validation types is the custom validator method. Just pass a function that returns the truth value for the incoming pincode number and our validation work is done. In the preceding example, we have checked whether the incoming pincode value (v) length is exactly 6, else let us throw an error that doesn't satisfy the condition. Even the error message can be customized using the message key.

4. Finally, we export the customer's collection schema using `module.exports` so that we can leverage it for our next steps.

5. When everything seems ready with the model, we are going to build our controller that can handle the incoming and outgoing data. Such operations are performed in `routes.js` and are provided in the following snippet:

```
{
  method: 'POST',
  path:'/customer/add',
  handler(request, h) {
      const requestBody = request.payload;
      return (async ()=>{
          try{
              /**
              * Native mongodb code
              * const dbInstance = request.dbInstance;
              * const customerCollection =
dbInstance.collection('customer');
              * return customerCollection.insert(requestBody)
              **/
              const customersModel = models.customers;
              const customersModelInstance = new
models.customers(requestBody);
              let error = new
models.customers_address(requestBody.Address).validateSync();
              if(error)
                  return Boom.boomify(error, { statusCode: 422 });

              await customersModelInstance.save();
              const customerList = await customersModel.find({});
              return {
                message : "customer added successfully",
                customerList
              };
              }catch(e){
              throw Boom.boomify(e, { statusCode: 500 });
          }
      })();
  }
}
```

The JavaScript object as shown is configuration for routes that consist of the request method, request URL, and the method in which we are going to construct the saving data logic, called a handler.

Let's take a look at the preceding code:

- `Models.customers` provides an instance of a customer schema. It is prototyped by all the mongoose methods that can be used in the request life cycle. We are using the `find` method in our case.
- Next, when the same `Models.customer` is instantiated with a new keyword and the payload as a parameter, the instance received provides payload as well as the payload manipulation methods such as `save`, `update`, or `delete`.
- We have used the `validateSync` method to validate our `pincode`. In our case, this operation is synchronous. For asynchronosity of code, we can simply use the `validate` method with callback.
- We have used Boom, a utility library, to handle the error response. It is strongly recommended by hapi.

 For more information on Boom, follow this link: `https://github.com/hapijs/boom`.

- As our code is asynchronous in nature, we have handled it with `async-await`. As stated by the new hapi v17, it is fully async/await end to end. Here the async/await methodology is the new way to handle asynchronousity across the framework. It gives much cleaner code to read as well as to write.
- Finally, we have returned a self-invoking function to the hapi handler.

Enough of the coding, let's run the app! We might need to restart our node server for working with respect to new changes. Stop the node service running in the Terminal using the *Ctrl + C* command. Start it again using `npm start`.

We also need to prepare the data in the browser client POSTMAN, to add new customer data in our collection. This can be done as follows:

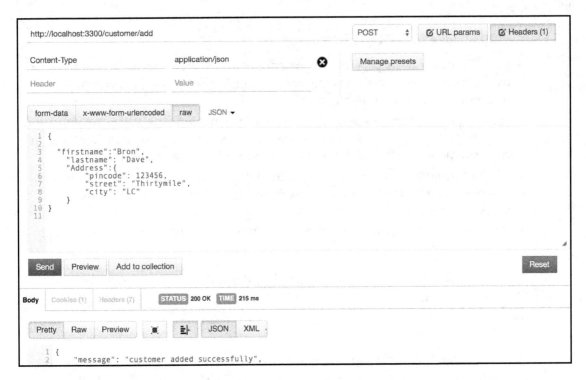

For more details on mongoose, here is the link: `http://mongoosejs.com/docs/guide.html`.

Summary

Congratulations! We are well on our way to being a full-stack JavaScript developer. Learning JSON implementations in different web development areas is an amazing journey. This chapter guided our learning curve to a new pinnacle by giving us an overall understanding of NoSQL database scripting. We started by setting up mongoDB and learning about BSON, then performed the basic operations on mongodb collections and, finally, successfully studied mongoose, an elegant object-modeling framework .

Our journey continues toward implementation of JSON by developing automation scripts or task runners for the application. Let's accomplish this in our next chapter.

10
Configuring the Task Runner Using JSON

Nowadays, phases such as unit testing, code integration, and creating a deployable optimized build are staple parts of the application development life cycle. Consider any code repository on GitHub: the community looks for test cases (especially the `specs.js` files) and the build status percentage (whether it's a pass or fail) before using any library or module. It is obvious that without such checksum tasks, a developer is not able to provide a benchmark for the stability and performance of any application module. In this chapter, we are going to learn about:

- What task runners are and why they are required
- What `gulp.js` is and what purpose it serves
- Performing unit testing using Mocha framework and `gulp.js`
- Automating all unit test cases using JSON configuration

So, let's get started!

What is a task runner?

In the context of web scripting, task runners are the libraries that help us to perform functionalities with ease and minimum effort. Task runners can help in doing the following:

- Minifying your client application JavaScript file to increase overall performance
- Configuring your app modules selection at build time
- Creating a build that only comprises a single `index.html` file, CSS, assets, and minified and uglified JavaScript on a single command
- Testing **BDD** (**behavior-driven data**) assertions

In this chapter, we are going to test our APIs individually using the default assertion library of Node, and we are going to automate them using the gulp task runner library. In `Chapter 9`, *Storing JSON Documents in MongoDB*, we created two APIs in our hapi application; now we are going to test them. Before creating the tasks, let's learn about `gulp.js`, what it is used for, and what its capabilities are.

Introducing gulp.js

`gulp.js` is basically a JavaScript task runner. All the tasks that were listed previously, as well as bundling of files, refreshing the browser automatically when you save a file after coding, running unit test files, and deploying a build with Amazon API, can be performed using `gulp.js`. `gulp.js` performs many tasks that are repetitive and boring:

> *"gulp is a toolkit for automating painful or time-consuming tasks in your development workflow, so you can stop messing around and build something"*
>
> *– gulpjs.com*

Let's take a look over the feature list and see why `gulp.js` is so much more awesome than other libraries, such as `grunt.js`, that are available in the open source market:

- Small, plugin-based structure design for implementing tasks
- Easy to read and understand the task
- Tasks can be integrated to perform automations
- All IO operations are performed using node.js streams, so all modifications are done in memory first and then written once at the end, resulting in faster and better performance
- Great community support and great contribution to the plugins ecosystem

Alright, now that we know why `gulp.js` is great, let's start with installation, then move on to coding. Here are the steps for installing `gulp.js`:

1. Create a gulp configuration file called `gulpfile.js` at the project root level. This will help to manage all the project files at root level. In our case, we are going to use the *hapi* app (`node-tes-app` directory) and the gulp configuration file at the same level. So, we already have a `Chapter 10`, *Configuring the Task Runner Using JSON*, folder in our github repo (`https://github.com/bron10/json-essentials-book`) to get an idea of the scaffolding.

2. Let's start by installing all the required packages using the following command:

```
$ npm install gulp-cli -g
$ npm install gulp --save-dev
```

The `gulp-cli` package enables us to use gulp for command-line interface purposes. Now that the installation is complete and `gulpfile.js` is ready, let's write some code in it.

Creating tasks in gulp.js

We are going to create a first task to greet our readers. Again, let us go through a simple stepwise procedure so that nothing is missed out.

1. First, let us write some pluggable code in `gulpfile.js`, as follows:

```
const gulp = require('gulp');
gulp.task('default', () => {
    console.log("Greetings to Readers!");
})
```

In preceding snippet, the task method of gulp module requires two parameters. The first one is name of task as a string and second parameter is callback where we can write the actual logic behind the specific task.

2. Go back to the Terminal and run the `gulp` command. You will receive the following output:

```
Last login: Mon Feb 19 12:45:11 on ttys009
brunos-MacBook-Pro:chapter 10 bruno$ gulp
[17:13:03] Using gulpfile ~/Documents/projects/js/book/json essential/codes/chapter 10/gulpfile.js
[17:13:03] Starting 'default'...
Greeting Readers!
[17:13:03] Finished 'default' after 155 µs
brunos-MacBook-Pro:chapter 10 bruno$
```

Now, let's add a little complexity by adding one more task and using it as a dependency to the previous one:

```
const gulp = require('gulp');

gulp.task('default', ['dependent-task'], () => {
    console.log("Greetings to Readers!");
})
```

```
gulp.task('dependent-task', () => {
    console.log("Greetings to all!");
})
```

3. On executing the preceding code using `gulp`, we get the following output:

```
brunos-MacBook-Pro:chapter 10 bruno$ gulp
[17:26:13] Using gulpfile ~/Documents/projects/js/book/json essential/codes/chapter 10/gulpfile.js
[17:26:13] Starting 'dependent-task'...
Greetings to all!
[17:26:13] Finished 'dependent-task' after 184 µs
[17:26:13] Starting 'default'...
Greetings to Readers!
[17:26:13] Finished 'default' after 108 µs
brunos-MacBook-Pro:chapter 10 bruno$
```

In the preceding output, `dependent-task` is executed before the `default` task. This can be verified in the preceding screenshot by checking the sequence of the statements logged by the `console.log` method. This confirms that we can use the strategy of dependent tasks to run the tasks in sequence.

Moving on, we are going to:

1. Write a unit test for an API
2. Run the API unit test using gulp

We are going to use the *hapi* app, which provides API endpoints, created in Chapter 9, *Storing JSON Documents in MongoDB*. Make sure that both MongoDB and our Node `app.js` services are running. Let's write a simple unit test that makes an API call and checks for data.

Writing a unit test

A unit test case is required to test a specific unit of code that offers some kind of functionality. In our case, we are planning to test a simple route or *hapi* app that greets our users. Let's divide our unit test case task into some measure code chunks so that we can get clarity on writing an appropriate unit test case:

1. Create a `routes.spec.js` file. The naming convention specifies the file that we are going to test, `routes.js`. It is recommended by our open source community to suffix the test file as `spec`.

2. We need to divide our unit tests cases with respect to all the routes present in routes.js and enclose our assertions in some test-driven code. An npm module called mocha.js can help us in this case. By the way, writing a set of code to accomplish and pass test cases is called **test-driven development** (TDD).

3. Let's install mocha using the following command:

```
npm i mocha --save-dev
```

4. To specify our unit case, we need to include the code in our spec file, shown as follows:

```
describe('Test routes', () => {
    it('Testing GET: greetings', () => {
        console.log("Testing the /greeting route");
    })
})
```

5. Now, run the following mocha test command:

```
$ ./node_modules/mocha/bin/mocha routes.specs.js
```

6. We should get the following output:

```
brunos-MacBook-Pro:chapter 10 bruno$ ./node_modules/mocha/bin/mocha routes.specs.js


  Test routes
Testing the /greeting route
    ✓ Testing GET: greetings


  1 passing (7ms)
```

Here, we prepared our test blocks so that they can consume the test scenarios. One more thing: the command to run a unit test spec file seems too big, doesn't it? We are going to minimize it by adding/altering the following script key inside the package.json at root level:

```
"scripts": {
  "test": "./node_modules/mocha/bin/mocha routes.specs.js"
}
```

1. Now, we just need to run the `npm test` command in the Terminal.

For more information on Mocha, follow this link: `https://mochajs.org/#getting-started`.

Next, we need one more awesome library that can request our API on execution of the `test` file. We are going to use the request node module available in the `npm` library:

2. Run command:

   npm install request --save-dev

3. Then, include the request module in our `routes.spec.js`, as follows.

   ```
   const request = require('request');
   ```

4. The request module instance fulfills all the impediments that we would require to complete an asynchronous HTTP request. For now, our minimal requirement would be a request URL, a request method, and the callback to handle the response. This can be shown as follows:

   ```
   const request = require('request');

   describe('Test routes', () => {
       it('Testing GET: greetings', () => {
           console.log("Testing the /greetings route");
       request.get('http://localhost:3300/greetings', (err, httpResponse,
   body) => {
               if (err) {
                   throw err;
               }
               console.log("statusCode", httpResponse.statusCode);
               console.log("body", body);
               done();
           })
       })
   })
   ```

5. Run using the `npm test` command and you should receive the following output:

```
brunos-MacBook-Pro:chapter 10 bruno$ npm test

> gulp-file@1.0.0 test /Users/bruno/Documents/projects/js/book/json essential/codes/chapter 10
> ./node_modules/mocha/bin/mocha routes.specs.js



  Test routes
Testing the /greetings route
    ✓ Testing GET: greetings


  1 passing (18ms)

statusCode 200
body hello readers
```

Note that we have received the status code as 200 and body as `hello readers`. The `done` parameter is a function used to run mocha for asynchronous code. On completion of asynchronous code, we need to invoke the done function, so we are going to invoke the done function inside the callback of our async request.

Now is the time to induce the power of the assertions library provided by the node.js API. Assertions provide a way to differentiate the expected data versus the actual data. Using assertions during development, we apply the BDD testing methodology to our application, reducing a wide range of bugs at development phase. Let's write few assertions, shown as follows:

```
const request = require('request');
const assert = require('assert');

describe('Test routes', () => {
    it('Testing GET: greetings', (done) => {
        console.log("Testing the /greetings route");
        request.get('http://localhost:3300/greetings', (err, httpResponse,
body) => {
            if (err) {
                throw err;
            }
            assert.equal(httpResponse.statusCode, 200);
            assert.ok(body == 'hello readers');
            done();
        })
    })
})
```

In the preceding code, we included the `assert` module provided by the Node API. The `assert.equal` method is used to check for the equality of two operands. In our case, we use it to check the response `statusCode` received with the expected status code of the HTTP response. It also accepts the third parameter as a message that can be displayed if the assertion fails. The `assert.ok` method checks requires a single truthy value as a parameter to complete a successful assertion. In our case, if the response body fails to respond as `hello reader`, our assertion shall fail.

Let's test for failure by modifying our expected `statuscode` input as `400`, which was originally `200`:

```
brunos-MacBook-Pro:chapter 10 bruno$ npm test

> gulp-file@1.0.0 test /Users/bruno/Documents/projects/js/book/json essential/codes/chapter 10
> ./node_modules/mocha/bin/mocha routes.specs.js


  Test routes
Testing the /greetings route
    1) Testing GET: greetings


  0 passing (29ms)
  1 failing

  1) Test routes
       Testing GET: greetings:

     Uncaught AssertionError [ERR_ASSERTION]: 200 == 400
     + expected - actual

     -200
     +400

     at Request.request.get [as _callback] (routes.specs.js:11:11)
     at Request.self.callback (node_modules/request/request.js:186:22)
     at Request.<anonymous> (node_modules/request/request.js:1163:10)
     at IncomingMessage.<anonymous> (node_modules/request/request.js:1085:12)
     at endReadableNT (_stream_readable.js:1056:12)
     at _combinedTickCallback (internal/process/next_tick.js:138:11)
     at process._tickCallback (internal/process/next_tick.js:180:9)
```

Great! Our unit test case is ready for the greeting API. Similarly, we can write an API unit test for the `/customer/add` API POST call, as follows:

```
it('Testing GET: customer/add', (done) => {
    console.log("Testing the /customer/add route");
    let payload = {
        "firstname": "firstTest",
        "lastname": "lastTest",
        "Address": {
            "pincode": 111111,
            "street": "testmile",
            "city": "TC"
        }
    };

    request.post({
        url: `http://localhost:3300/customer/add`,
        json: payload
    }, (err, httpResponse, body) => {
        if (err) {
            throw err;
        }
        const filteredCustomerList =
body.customerList.filter(function(customerData) {
            return (customerData.firstname == payload.firstname &&
customerData.lastname == payload.lastname)
        })

        assert.equal(httpResponse.statusCode, 200);
        //The data inserted above should have atleast one customer instance
        assert.ok(filteredCustomerList.length > 1);
        done();
    })
})

assert.equal(httpResponse.statusCode, 200);
  //The data inserted above should have atleast one customer instance
  assert.ok(filteredCustomerList.length > 1);
  done();
  })
})
```

In the preceding code snippet, we are familiar with our first assertion. The second assertion states that at least one instance inserted in the customer list collection using the API endpoints should be present. In this scenario, the instance matches the instance of a customer, which is fetched by `firstname` and `lastname`.

On running the preceding code, we receive the following output, which states that two test scenarios are passed:

```
brunos-MacBook-Pro:chapter 10 bruno$ npm test

> gulp-file@1.0.0 test /Users/bruno/Documents/projects/js/book/json essential/codes/chapter 10
> ./node_modules/mocha/bin/mocha routes.specs.js



  Test routes
Testing the /greetings route
    ✓ Testing GET: greetings
Testing the /customer/add route
    ✓ Testing GET: customer/add


  2 passing (35ms)
```

Our unit tests are ready. We are going to integrate them as a single gulp task to test the routes. Gulp has a great plugin library, and we are going to use gulp-mocha for the integration. Let's install using the following command:

```
npm install gulp-mocha --save-dev
```

Let's focus on gulpfile.js and create a new task, as follows:

```
gulp.task('test-routes', function() {
    return gulp.src('./routes.specs.js')
        .pipe(mochaPlugin({ reporter: 'spec' }))
});
```

To use mochaPlugin, we need to include it at the beginning in our gulpfile.js, as follows:

```
const mochaPlugin = require('gulp-mocha');
```

We also need to note that we have used the pipe method, which effectively passes the source stream of our specs file to mochaPlugin so that it may perform the tests.

On running the gulp test-routes command, our unit testing is performed by gulp. Amazing! Now we are going to use dependency strategies to create some awesome automation in the next section.

Automation testing

By integrating the power of `gulp` plugins and `gulp` task together, we can create a flow of consecutive tasks that can run parallel or sequentially as per our requirements. Though we have the gulp task dependency feature, we are going to use the npm `run-sequence` module to run the task in sequence. This helps us to structure the task easily and reduce the complexity when the number of tasks increases over time.

Run the following command to install `run-sequence`:

```
npm install run-sequence --save-dev
```

With respect to its usage, the only thing we need to remember is that every gulp task should either return a stream or promise, or should be handled using callback. Let's justify this statement and leverage the power of gulp automation by creating three simple tasks in a flow:

1. Start our *hapi* app.
2. Test the API of the *hapi* app. While testing, make sure the `test-node-app` directory is present at the root level of `gulpfile.js`. Refer to the `Chapter 10`, *Configuring the Task Runner Using JSON*, code GitHub repository for more help (`https://github.com/bron10/json-essentials-book`).
3. Stop the *hapi* app.

   Here is the code snippet for these tasks:

```
const gulp = require('gulp');
const mochaPlugin = require('gulp-mocha');
const runSequence = require('run-sequence');
var exec = require('child_process').exec;
let processInstance = undefined;

gulp.task('default', ['dependent-task'], () => {
    console.log("Greetings to Readers!");
})

gulp.task('dependent-task', () => {
    console.log("Greetings to all!");
})

//Start our hapi app
gulp.task('start-app', (cb) => {
    //Update the package.json for start script
    processInstance = exec(`npm start`);
```

```
        cb();
})

//Test the API of the hapi app
gulp.task('test-routes', () => {
    return gulp.src('./routes.specs.js').pipe(mochaPlugin({ reporter:
'spec' }))
});

//Stop the hapi app
gulp.task('stop-app', (cb) => {
    processInstance.kill(0);
    process.exit(0);
    cb();
})
gulp.task('Test-API-Flow', function() {
    return runSequence('start-app', 'test-routes', 'stop-app');
});
```

In the preceding gulp tasks, we have either completed the task using the `gulp` callback parameter `cb` or returned the stream. This is required by the `runSequence` function so that it may know the completion of each task before the next one starts.

Let's go through all the new tasks one by one:

- `start-app`: This task is responsible for starting the hapi server instance by running the `npm start` command. The command is scripted in `package.json` of `gulpfile.js` instead of the `test-node-app` directory, as `gulpfile.js` is situated at the root level where we are currently executing commands in the Terminal. The command also uses the `exec` method of the `child_process` module provided by node.js API, which spawns a new sub process of its parent `gulp` process.
- `test-routes`: This is the `gulp` task for testing the hapi API routes.
- `stop-app`: This is a `gulp` task that elegantly shuts down both the processes (the application process as well as the `gulp` process).
- `Test-API-Flow`: This `gulp` task merely sequences all the preceding tasks.

 Before executing, make sure that you are not running a server instance already. Be sure to exit other node processes (especially the hapi server process) before starting the `gulp` process. You may get an **eaddrinuse** error.

Run `gulp Test-API-Flow` and check the automation magic inside the Terminal, as shown in following screenshot:

```
brunos-MacBook-Pro:chapter 10 bruno$ gulp Test-API-Flow
[12:19:18] Using gulpfile ~/Documents/projects/js/book/json essential/codes/chapter 10/gulpfile.js
[12:19:18] Starting 'Test-API-Flow'...
[12:19:18] Starting 'start-app'...
[12:19:18] Finished 'start-app' after 4.89 ms
[12:19:18] Starting 'test-routes'...
[12:19:18] Finished 'Test-API-Flow' after 17 ms


  Test routes
Testing the /greetings route
    ✓ Testing GET: greetings
Testing the /customer/add route
    ✓ Testing GET: customer/add


  2 passing (38ms)

[12:19:19] Finished 'test-routes' after 477 ms
[12:19:19] Starting 'stop-app'...
brunos-MacBook-Pro:chapter 10 bruno$
```

Gulp JSON configuration

Last but not least, we need to configure our gulp task using JSON. Let's create a JSON config file named `gulpconfig.json`. The `gulpconfig.json` file will provide control over all the settings, sources, and naming of tasks from a single location. Even though we have one single route API task to test for now, it is best to start it in an advanced stage. Once the application API increases, it becomes difficult to change something at the app structure level. Here are the contents of `gulpconfig` file:

```json
{
    "apiflow":
    {
        "name": "Test-API-Flow",
        "sequence": ["start-app", "test-routes", "stop-app"]
    },
    "routes":
    {
        "name": "test-routes",
        "src": "./routes.specs.js"
    }
}
```

Now we need to modify the following task in our `gulpfile.js`, as shown:

```
//Test the API of the hapi app
gulp.task(gulpTasksConfig.routes.name, () => {
    return gulp.src(gulpTasksConfig.routes.src).pipe(mochaPlugin({
reporter: 'spec' }))
});

gulp.task(gulpTasksConfig.apiflow.name, function() {
    return runSequence(...gulpTasksConfig.apiflow.sequence);
});
```

In the preceding code, we have used the `gulpTaskConfig` instance of the config file. Make sure that you include the following at the beginning in `gulpfile.js`:

```
const gulpTasksConfig = require('./gulpconfig.json');
```

In above code we are learning a new technique of segregating the array values as a parameter over the `runSequence` function invocation. The operator is called as spread operator notify by three consecutive dots . . . prefixed to the config key called as sequence which provides an array.

Summary

The study of JSON drives us toward various developmental phases. In this chapter, we learned about unit testing and automation. We used `gulp.js`, which proved to be an incredible task runner tool. We learned about two important concepts of unit testing: BDD testing using the node.js assertion library; and `mocha.js`, the TDD framework for JavaScript apps.

It is highly recommended to unit test as much as we can. This reduces bugs to a great extent and provides maintainability of code over time. As the saying goes:

"If you don't like unit testing your product, most likely your customers won't like to test it either."

– Anonymous

Moving forward in next chapter, things are going to be more interesting when we are going to study about JSON implementation in the realtime system followed by distributed ones.

11
JSON for Real-Time and Distributed Data

Until now, we have worked on RESTful http API endpoints as sources of data communication between the client and server. An http request has proved to be the best way to have reliable data availability. The only hurdle can be the response time if there are some issues with network latency. What if we don't want to wait for the server response to be received, or we need the data to be received in real time? Consider the scenario of some simple messaging activity with some product bot, or a screen cast for a presentation that is delivered to workplace staff from home. The only criteria for success in this case is the data availability on time and its correctness. One web technology protocol that provides real-time solutions to such scenarios is **WebSocket**.

Another important thing we hear a lot about is the distributed system. Once a web application is deployed and live, somewhere down the line we need to scale our network resources for data consistency and increase the quality of communication between the distant nodes. In such scenarios, distributed system solutions serve the purpose of managing data over the network. In this chapter, we are going to learn about **Apache Kafka**, which provides a scalable stream-processing system.

Here is an overview of the topics covered in this chapter:

- Real-time communication using JSON with Socket.IO
- Setting up the Socket.IO server and its clients
- Introduction to distributed systems using JSON with Apache Kafka
- Installing Apache and implementing the distributed system concepts in a real-time application

Using JSON with Socket.IO

Setting up the `Socket.IO` server is simple. Here is the procedure to implement a real-time server that provides a continuous HTTP handshake, and continues to listen to requests via the Socket.IO framework.

We are going to demonstrate the implementation of JSON for real-time via a *pinboard* app. Any anonymous user who connects to the real-time server joins the session, and can view the *pinboard* and add whatever thoughts or whatever else that they like.

We are going to divide our application into two phases :

1. Designing the board
2. Implementing the real-time functionality via the `Socket.IO` library

Designing the board

In this phase, we are going to design a web interface through which our user can add or view the pins on the board. Remember how in Chapter 7, *Alternate Implementations of JSON*, we learned about template embedding? We are going to use a similar technique for our *pinboard*. So, let's start by creating a template file called `index.html.js` and inserting the following HTML elements:

```
//index.html.js
module.exports = `
<!DOCTYPE html>
<html>
    <head>
    <title>Pin board</title>
    </head>
    <style>
        body{
```

```
        background-color: #CCB;
    }
    .card {
        /* Add shadows to create the "card" effect */
        box-shadow: 0 4px 8px 0 rgba(0,0,0,0.2);
        transition: 0.3s;
        width: 30%;
        background-color:white;
        float: left;
        margin: 5px;
    }
    .card:hover {
        box-shadow: 0 8px 16px 0 rgba(0,0,0,0.2);
    }

    .container {
        padding: 2px 16px;
    }
    h4{
        text-align: right;
    }
    textarea{
        border: 0; padding: 10px; width: 90%; margin-right: .5%;
        float: left;
        width : 60%;
    }
    input{
        float : left;
        width : 15%;
        padding: 15px;
    }
    button{
        padding: 15px;
        float: left;
        width : 20%;
    }
</style>
<body>
<textarea autocomplete="off" id="textData"></textarea><button
  id="postButton">Post</button>
    <div class="collection">
        <div class="card">
            <div class="container">
                <p>Lorem Ipsum is simply dummy text of the printing and
typesetting industry. Lorem Ipsum has been the industry's standard dummy
text ever since the 1500s, when an unknown printer took a galley of type
and scrambled it to make a type specimen book. It has survived not only
five centuries, but also the leap into electronic typesetting, remaining
```

```
essentially unchanged. It was popularised in the 1960s with the release of
Letraset sheets containing Lorem Ipsum passages, and more recently with
desktop publishing software like Aldus PageMaker including versions of
Lorem Ipsum.
                    </p>
                <h4><b>John Doe</b></h4>
            </div>
        </div>
    </div>
</body>
</html>
`;
```

The preceding template contains all the UI elements required for our *pinboard* app. In the preceding code, we exported a simple string that consists of all the HTML, with textarea as the input element, the button with text Post as the action element, and the collection class, which will hold the new pins or cards on the board. Moving further, let's set up the server so that we can render the template at the browser's request.

Setting up the Socket.IO server

The WebSocket implementation is wrapped and handled with an amazing library called Socket.IO. It is not just a library, but a framework that provides so many more features than just a library. Moving on, let's install Socket.IO using the following command:

```
npm install socket.io --save
```

Now, we need to render the template in the browser upon a request to the node server. To do so, add the following snippet to our app.js:

```
const templateData = require('./index.html');
const server = require('http').createServer((req, res) => {
    res.setHeader('content-type', 'text/html');
    res.end(templateData);
});
const io = require('socket.io')(server);
io.on('connection', function(client) {
    client.on('disconnect', function() {
        console.log('user disconnected');
    });
    console.log("connected to realtime data server");
});
server.listen(3400);
```

Before going ahead with an explanation of preceding code, let's check whether our server provides the required view when we browse for `http://localhost:3400`. Here is the output:

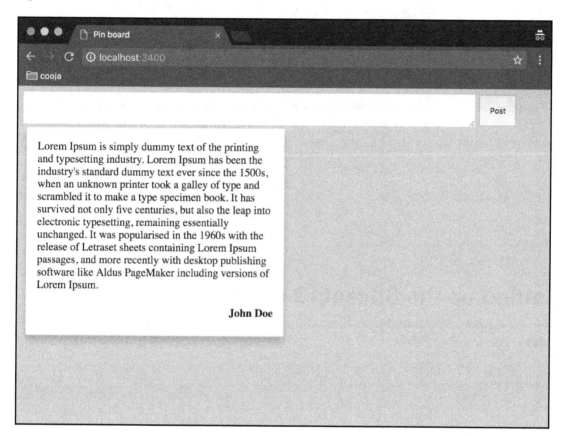

How Socket.IO works

Let's walk through the code line by line. We imported the `index.html.js` template, which is a simple node module that exports string-based HTML data. Then, we created an HTTP server to handle the HTTP request and response via a web browser or any other client that renders an HTML view.

We created a real-time server by passing an instance of the server to the required `Socket.IO` library. `Socket.IO` is the crude library for our real-time app. It provides a wrapper to WebSocket. WebSocket is a protocol that performs a continuous communication handshake over **TCP** (**transmission control protocol**).

To put it into simple terms, once the client establishes the connection to the WebSocket server, the client doesn't have to make a specific request to get particular data each time. Once the first request for a connection is established, the client can receive continuous data with respect to time (looping and emitting) and any other event triggers. The client or server just needs to trigger an event for passing the data and listen via a callback to receive the data. This event model is leveraged using the **pubsub (publish-subscribe)** pattern, or to be more specific, using listeners. In the preceding code, we have two listeners: connection and disconnect.

We will understand all of this more precisely once we go through the following code snippet. In app.js, we are going to add a new listener named as connection that will listen to a disconnect event. This is as shown in following code:

```
io.on('connection', (client) => {
    console.log("connected to realtime data server");
    client.on('disconnect', () => {
        console.log("A user is disconnected!");
    })
});
```

Setting up the Socket.IO client

Now we are going to connect our client, index.html.js, to the Socket.IO server by adding a client-side script, as follows:

```
<script src="/socket.io/socket.io.js"></script>
<script>
const socket = io();
</script>
```

Just add the about script tag after the end of the body tag. socket.io.js handles the connection to the server on invoking the io prototype method. By default, it establishes the connection with the same URL through which the socket file was served to browser. It also provides an option to set the connection URL differently by passing it as a URL string parameter.

Once the connection and disconnect listeners are implemented and the client is also connected, on the browser refresh, we will receive the log, as follows:

connected to realtime data server
A user is disconnected!

Now, let's add some functionality so that we can capture the user input and put it on our *pinboard*. We are going to use the jQuery library, which will make our UI-related code easy. For readers who don't know jQuery, it is client-script JavaScript library that provides manipulation of DOM elements with ease. We include the jQuery library as follows:

```
<script src="http://code.jquery.com/jquery-3.3.1.slim.min.js"
integrity="sha256-3edrmyuQ0w65f8gfBsqowzjJe2iM6n0nKciPUp8y+7E="
crossorigin="anonymous" />
```

You need to place it above our custom script tag, so that we can access the global variable of jQuery $, which provides all the methods.

By now, we have some idea of how things work as event listeners. It is time to learn about making decisions as to how many listeners we actually need and on what basis we can fulfill such decisions:

1. Figure out the direction of data flow. Is it single-way or a dual-way communication? This can be discovered by capturing the input data from the browser text area and sending it to server. The server can persist the data (temporarily, for now) and send it to all the subscribed clients (browsers). This can be demonstrated by following code:

```
//index.html.js
$(function() {
    const socket = io();

    $("#postButton").on('click', function(e) {
        let textData = $("#textData").val();
        let writtenBy = $("#writtenBy").val();
        socket.emit('new-pin', { story: textData, writtenBy:
         writtenBy });
        $("#textData").val('');
        $("#writtenBy").val('');
        return false;
    })

    socket.on('append-to-list', function(data) {
        console.log("data", data);
        $('.collection').append('<div class="card"><div
        class="container"><p>' +
        data.story + '</p><h4><b>' + data.writtenBy + '</b></h4>
        </div></div>')
    })
})
```

To summarize the preceding code, we attached a click event on the element with an id of `postButton`, which is an HTML button. Then, we extracted data from inputs such as the name and the text to be posted and emitted through the WebSocket (`ws://`) protocol, using `new-pin` as the channel. It is expected that a subscriber will be created that will be listening to the new-pin channel on the server side.

2. Let's implement the subscriber in `app.js`:

```
let pinBoard = [];

io.on('connection', (client) => {
    console.log("connected to realtime data server");
    client.on('disconnect', () => {
        console.log("A user is disconnected!");
    })

    client.on('new-pin', (pinData) => {
        pinBoard.push(pinData);
    })
});
```

In preceding snippet, the changes are clear. We created a temporary storage array, `pinBoard`, to store all the data on the board just for our reference. As soon as we receive `new-pin` data, we push it to `pinBoard`. Note that there is no way to update the UI for now.

3. Here comes our next step. To remember every subscriber or listener, there must be an emitter. When a block is missed or fails to function, the communication cannot be complete. To prevent this, we need to update the UI pin list by emitting the pin data in turn, so that all the clients that are subscribed can receive the updates. This is done as follows:

```
client.on('new-pin', (pinData) => {
    pinBoard.push(pinData);
    io.emit('append-to-list', pinData)
})
```

We create a new channel or namespace called `append-to-list`. On invocation of the `client.emit` method over at the append-to-list namespace, it will send the data to the subscriber's listener callback. So without further ado, let's create a listener at our client code in `index.html.js`, as follows.

```
socket.on('append-to-list', function(data) {
    $('.collection').append('<div class="card">
    <div class="container"><p>' +
    data.story + '</p><h4><b>' + data.writtenBy +
    '</b></h4></div></div>')
})
```

That's it! Let's check whether, if we add a new story or message to our `pinboard`, the `pinboard` is updated in two different browser tabs. Run the `node app.js` command and you should get the following output in browser by connecting to `http://localhost:3400`:

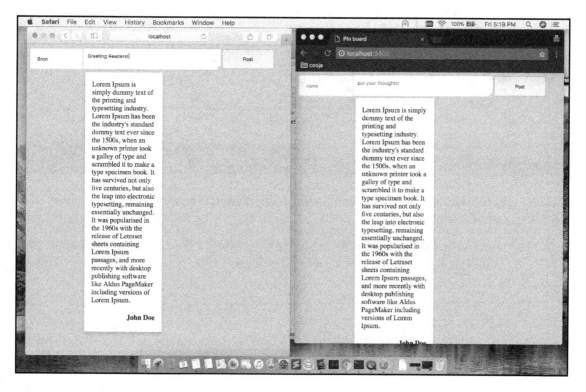

The preceding screenshot contains two browsers side by side. The user is typing a new post.Both the browsers lets say client are connected to the pinboard server app. Let us check the results of action the client, when the user clicks on the post button. following is the screenshot representing post-click state:

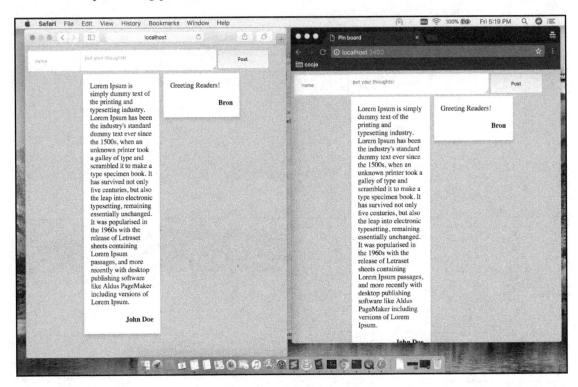

As shown in preceding screenshot both the browser client has received the same expected post. This can be a useful.

4. Now, we are going to handle the default dummy `pinboard` data at our client as well the server code with the logic, as follows:

```
io.on('connection', (client) => {
    console.log("connected to realtime data server");
    io.emit('pin-list', pinBoard)
    client.on('disconnect', () => {
        console.log("A user is disconnected!");
    })

    client.on('new-pin', (pinData) => {
        pinBoard.push(pinData);
```

```
            console.log("pinData", pinData);
            io.emit('append-to-list', pinData)
      })
  });
```

In the preceding code, we sent the `pinboard` data by default over the pin-list channel. This is done so that the pin-list data is handled dynamically.

5. In `index.html.js`, remove the `div` element that has `card` as a class name with all of its content and move it to the jQuery code, so that it can be appended to the collection class element only if the `pinboard` data is not present by default when receiving in the pin-list channel. The modifications are shown in the following code of `index.html.js`:

```
//index.html.js
module.exports = `
<!DOCTYPE html>
<html>
<head>
  <title>Pin board</title>
</head>
<style>
body{
  background-color: #CCB;
}
.card {
    /* Add shadows to create the "card" effect */
    box-shadow: 0 4px 8px 0 rgba(0,0,0,0.2);
    transition: 0.3s;
    width: 30%;
    background-color:white;
    float: left;
    margin: 5px;
}
.card:hover {
    box-shadow: 0 8px 16px 0 rgba(0,0,0,0.2);
}

.container {
    padding: 2px 16px;
}
h4{
  text-align: right;
}
textarea{
  border: 0; padding: 10px; width: 90%; margin-right: .5%;
  float: left;
```

```css
    width : 50%;
}
input{
  float : left;
  width : 15%;
  padding: 15px;
}
button{
  padding: 15px;
    float: left;
    width : 20%;
}
</style>
<body>
  <input type="text" id="writtenBy" placeholder="name"/><textarea
   id="textData"
autocomplete="off" placeholder="put your thoughts!"></textarea>
<button
id="postButton">Post</button>
  <div class="collection">
  </div>
</body>
    <script
   src="http://code.jquery.com/jquery-3.3.1.slim.min.js"
   integrity="sha256-3edrmyuQ0w65f8gfBsqowzjJe2iM6n0nKciPUp8y+7E="
   crossorigin="anonymous"></script>
    <script src="/socket.io/socket.io.js"></script>
  <script>
    $(function () {

        const socket = io();
      $("#postButton").on('click', function(e){
        let textData = $("#textData").val();
        let writtenBy = $("#writtenBy").val();
        socket.emit('new-pin', {story : textData, writtenBy
        :writtenBy});
        $("#textData").val('');
        $("#writtenBy").val('');
        return false;
      })
      socket.on('append-to-list', function(data){
        $('.collection').append('<div class="card"><div
        class="container">   <p>'+data.story+'</p><h4>
      <b>'+data.writtenBy+'</b></h4></div></div>')
      })
      /**
       * Pin-list get all the pins on load
       */
```

```
    socket.on('pin-list', function(list){
      console.log("list", list);
      if(list.length){
        list.forEach(function(data){
    $('.collection').append('<div class="card"><div
    class="container">
    <p>'+data.story+'</p><h4><b>'+data.writtenBy+'</b></h4>
    </div></div>')
        })
      }else{
        $('.collection').append('<div class="card"><div
        class="container">      <p>Lorem Ipsum is simply dummy
         text of the printing and typesetting
        industry. Lorem Ipsum has been the standard dummy text ever
        since the 1500s, when an unknown printer took a galley of
type and
        scrambled it to make a type specimen book. It has survived
not only five
        centuries, but also the leap into electronic typesetting,
remaining
        essentially unchanged. It was popularised in the 1960s with
the release
        of Letraset sheets containing Lorem Ipsum passages, and more
recently
        with desktop publishing software like Aldus PageMaker
including versions
        of Lorem Ipsum.</p><h4><b>John Doe</b></h4></div></div>')
      }
    })
  })
    </script>
  </html>
```

6. Finally, restart the node app and connect to `http://localhost:3400` again. The output remains same but the pin list is handled properly:

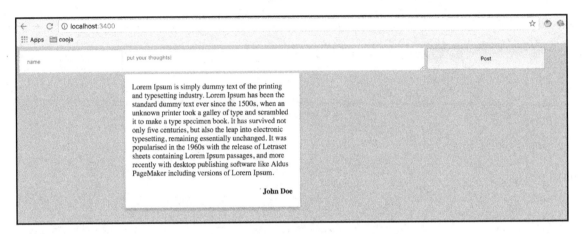

Woot! Our real-time app using JSON data is ready for launch. Some benefits that `Socket.IO` gives are smooth fallback for long polling if WebSockets are not supported, and simplification of the overall implementation of WebSockets, leveraging its maximum usage on the server side as well as the client side.

We have studied JSON implementation in a real-time application, Now, let's move on to JSON implementation for distributed systems.

Using JSON with Apache Kafka

Distributed systems are the logical systems that are segregated over a network. Leveraging the power of a distributed system normally starts in the stage where the application wants to scale horizontally over a network and when the flow of data is increasing over time. Let's refer to the flow of data as streams.

Kafka is a distributed stream processing platform that acts as a broker to producers and consumers of streams. In the world of Kafka, a producer is any entity that provides data, and a consumer is any entity that receives data.

Such a platform is really useful in various fields, such as stock markets and geo-spatial applications, where data is continuously produced and consumed.

We are going to study Apache Kafka by communicating JSON data via the simple real-time application that we implemented before. To do so, we need to learn a few more keywords from the following simple block diagram:

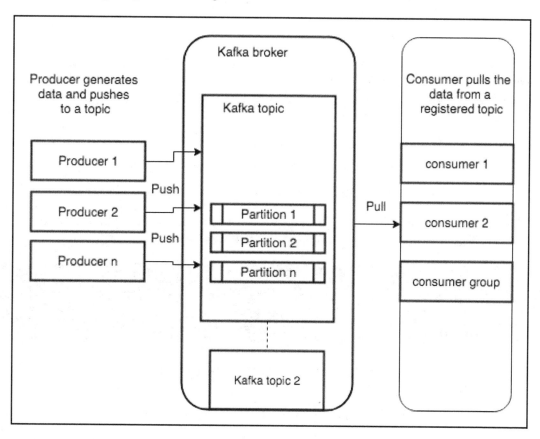

The preceding block diagram shows the basic streams in Kafka. The Kafka broker is tightly coupled with Zookeeper. We shall learn about Zookeeper in the next section.

Setting up Apache Kafka

We can download Apache Kafka from the following link: http://kafka.apache.org/ downloads . Note that Unix-based and Windows-based systems have different procedures for installation. Here is the best source that is recommended for Windows users: https:// medium.com/@shaaslam/installing-apache-kafka-on-windows-495f6f2fd3c8.

Getting back to the Unix system, we need to extract the `kafka_2.11-1.0.0.tgz` bundle. Our downloaded file is in the Downloads directory. Let's navigate to the directory and complete our procedure by using following commands:

```
$ cd ~/Downloads/
$ tar -xvf kafka_2.11-1.0.0.tgz
```

Once all the files are extracted, we are ready to get started with Kafka. Here is the procedure for starting the Kafka server:

1. Navigate to the directory:

    ```
    $ cd kafka_2.11-1.0.0
    ```

2. Start an instance of `zookeeper` using the following command:

    ```
    $ bin/zookeeper-server-start.sh config/zookeeper.properties
    ```

    Make sure that the `zookeeper` service is continuously running and is not exited in between steps. A sample screenshot is shown here:

```
Last login: Fri Feb 23 11:43:05 on ttys007
brunos-MacBook-Pro:kafka_2.11-1.0.0 bruno$ bin/zookeeper-server-start.sh config/zookeeper.properties
[2018-02-24 07:26:40,552] INFO Reading configuration from: config/zookeeper.properties (org.apache.zookeeper.server.quorum.QuorumPeerConfig)
[2018-02-24 07:26:40,554] INFO autopurge.snapRetainCount set to 3 (org.apache.zookeeper.server.DatadirCleanupManager)
[2018-02-24 07:26:40,554] INFO autopurge.purgeInterval set to 0 (org.apache.zookeeper.server.DatadirCleanupManager)
[2018-02-24 07:26:40,554] INFO Purge task is not scheduled. (org.apache.zookeeper.server.DatadirCleanupManager)
[2018-02-24 07:26:40,554] WARN Either no config or no quorum defined in config, running in standalone mode (org.apache.zookeeper.server.quorum.QuorumPeerMain
)
[2018-02-24 07:26:40,576] INFO Reading configuration from: config/zookeeper.properties (org.apache.zookeeper.server.quorum.QuorumPeerConfig)
[2018-02-24 07:26:40,577] INFO Starting server (org.apache.zookeeper.server.ZooKeeperServerMain)
```

3. Finally, start the Kafka service using the following command in a new Terminal or command prompt:

    ```
    $ bin/kafka-server-start.sh config/server.properties
    ```

The output of the preceding command provides a log of configuration, provided in the config directory, followed by its connection with Zookeeper.

What is Zookeeper? Why is it used? How is it different from pure Kafka?

There might be such questions in the minds of our readers. Coordinating between programs running on different machines with the aim of accomplishing some functionality for an application is a tough job. Zookeeper is an open source service provider that yields a simple coordination mechanism between distributed systems. Consider an example: say we have two servers with a Zookeeper instance named broker 1 and another Zookeeper instance named broker 2. If broker 1 configured as master from the start and broker 1 fails, the Zookeeper centralized service manages the election of a new broker.

Kafka on its own is a simple messaging system that provides a pubsub model of implementation. It is also a queuing system with temporary databases. Consider an example: say we want to develop a system that handles critical data but not actually in real-time like sending of emails. In such cases, we can rely on Kafka and push jobs onto kafka broker. The worker programs pull jobs as required and send emails. That's the basic idea. Integrating Kafka with Zookeeper doubles the strengths by managing a messaging system plus real-time streams processing plus distributed system coordinates. Hence, when we learn about Kafka, there is no point to not integrating Zookeeper into it; they are tightly coupled. Kafka depends on Zookeeper for persistent storage too. When we started Kafka using the command in preceding section, it established a connection with Zookeeper and selected a master.

Zookeeper in turn manages the Kafka clusters and keeps track of topics, messages, and more. For more information on Zookeeper, visit `http://zookeeper.apache.org/`, and for Kafka, visit `https://kafka.apache.org/`
.

Implementing Kafka with a Socket.IO application

We are going to implement a simple JSON message-passing functionality in our real-time app via Kafka. We are planning to send random messages over a specific time duration to Kafka. All the consumers that are registered to Kafka will be receiving our message. As a receiver, we are going to use our real-time *pinboard* application, hence keeping the implementation as simple as possible.

Let's understand the application flow and Kafka's basic nuts and bolts:

1. We will be creating a new file called `kafka-app.js` to segregate the Kafka implemented version.

2. Next, we will be installing `kafka-node` as a node client for Kafka. It also provides an integration with Zookeeper. Here is the command to install `kafka-node`:

   npm install kafka-node --save

3. Include our kafka-app.js, as follows:

   const kafka = require('kafka-node');

4. One step that we are missing as a dependency to start the Kafka broker for messaging passing is the creation of the topics. So, connecting to the Kafka instance, we are going to check whether a topic called `pinBoard` is already created; if not, then we will create one. This can be done as in following code snippet:

```
const kafkaClient = new kafka.Client();

kafkaClient.once('connect', function() {
    kafkaClient.loadMetadataForTopics([], function(error, results) {
        if (error) {
            return console.error(error);
        }
        let listofTopics = Object.keys(results[1]['metadata']);
        if (listofTopics.indexOf('pinBoard') == -1) {
            producer.createTopics(['pinBoard'], (err, data) => {
            console.log("New 'pinBoard' Topic created", err, data);
                //sendMessage();
            });
        } else {
            //sendMessage()
        }
    });
```

```
});
```

The preceding code consists of the following actions:

1. We establish a connection to Kafka.
2. We get all the information regarding existing metadata using
   `kafkaClient.loadMetadataForTopics`.
3. If the `pinBoard` topic doesn't exist in the received response, we create one.
4. Now is the time to create a producer that will produce an input. We have a JSON
   file with about 10 inputs, which are sent to Kafka every minute. Get the JSON file
   from the following GitHub repository link: `https://github.com/bron10/json-`
   `essentials-book/blob/master/chapter%2011/story.json`. Let's include the
   JSON file as follows:

```
const storyJSON = require('./story.json');
```

Here is the producer function:

```
function sendMessage() {
    let count = -1;
    setInterval(() => {
        count = count == 9 ? count = 0 : ++count;
        /**
            * [messages multi messages can be an array,
            * single message can be a string or
            * a JSON]
            */
        producer.send([{
            topic: 'pinBoard',
            messages: JSON.stringify(storyJSON[count]),
        }], (err, data) => {
            console.log("Message send by producer", err, data);
        })
    }, 60000)
}
```

5. To use the `producer` instance in the preceding code, we need to create one using
   following code in the initialization section at the start:

```
const producer = new kafka.Producer(kafkaClient);
```

6. Once the `producer` instance is ready to use, we are going to use `producer.send()` method to send the message data to the Kafka broker. Note that this is an asynchronous method, so we are going to pass a second parameter as a callback. The preceding code snippet also includes a logic to reset the counter after the tenth element in the JSON.

Also, we need to handle any errors that may occur. Kafka client module also provides an event listener for handling the error that may occur while in either of the producer-broker-consumer state, as follows:

```
producer.on('error', function(err) {
    console.log('Producer is in error state');
    console.log(err);
})
```

7. Now, we are going to uncomment the `sendMessage()` invocation. Also, make sure that both Kafka services are already running. If not, start Zookeeper as well as Kafka and then run the `kafka-app.js` file using the following command:

```
node kafka-app.js
```

You should get the following output:

```
brunos-MacBook-Pro:chapter 11 bruno$ node kafka-app.js
Producer will send message at every interval of 1 min
 Waiting for 1 min...
Message send by producer null { pinBoard: { '0': 23 } }
```

In the preceding steps, we have successfully created a Kafka producer and saved the data to Kafka. To check the real-time updates and whether the consumers receive any data, you can connect to Kafka consumer shell using the following command:

```
$ bin/kafka-console-consumer.sh --bootstrap-server localhost:9092 --topic
pinBoard --from-beginning
```

If your Kafka contains an older version of Zookeeper, make sure you pass one more mandatory parameter as—`zookeeper <urls>` in the preceding execution of the consumer configuration command. The `urls` consist of a host and a port, which provide the Zookeeper connection. There can be multiple URLs to handle broker failures.

The preceding command yields the following output:

```
brunos-MacBook-Pro:kafka_2.11-1.0.0 bruno$ bin/kafka-console-consumer.sh --bootstrap-server localhost:9092 --topic pinBoard --from-beginning

{"story":"You cannot shake hands with a clenched fist","writtenBy":"Indira Gandhi"}
{"story":"When you reach the end of your rope","writtenBy":"tie a knot in it and hang on"}
{"story":"Learning never exhausts the mind","writtenBy":"Leonardo da Vinci"}
{"story":"You cannot shake hands with a clenched fist","writtenBy":"Indira Gandhi"}
{"story":"When you reach the end of your rope","writtenBy":"tie a knot in it and hang on"}
{"story":"No act of kindness, no matter how small","writtenBy":"Aesop"}
{"story":"When you reach the end of your rope.. tie a knot in it and hang on","writtenBy":"Franklin D. Roosevelt"}
{"story":"But man is not made for defeat. A man can be destroyed but not defeated","writtenBy":"Ernest Hemingway"}
{"story":"When you reach the end of your rope.. tie a knot in it and hang on","writtenBy":"Franklin D. Roosevelt"}
{"story":"There is nothing permanent except change","writtenBy":"Heraclitus"}
{"story":"You cannot shake hands with a clenched fist","writtenBy":"Indira Gandhi"}
{"story":"Learning never exhausts the mind","writtenBy":"Leonardo da Vinci"}
```

Implementing the Kafka consumer

Moving on, let's implement the consumer concepts to our real-time app. This will complete our JSON message-passing implementation using Kafka. We are going to work on `app.js` for now, as it is a consumer for us:

1. Firstly, we need to create a consumer that will connect to a Kafka client on port `9092`, which is the default port:

```
const kafka = require('kafka-node'),
    client = new kafka.Client(),
    consumer = new kafka.Consumer(client,
        [{ topic: 'pinBoard', offset: 0 }],
        {
            autoCommit: false
        }
    );
```

Here, we have created a consumer instance that connects to Kafka with topics that are passed as array parameters to the `kafka.Consumer` method.

2. Create an error handler that will manage all the errors at the consumer side. This can be done using the following code:

```
consumer.on('error', function (err) {
    console.log('Error:',err);
})
```

3. Once our `consumer` instance is ready, we are going to listen to all the messages that are pulled by consumers. Just a gentle reminder: in Kafka, consumers pull the messages, which means that the Kafka service does not send them explicitly as in a ping-pong server. That is the difference with respect to real-time implementation as in a *Socket.IO* app.

   The code for this is shown as follows:

```
consumer.on('message', function(message) {
    console.log("consumer message-->", (message));
    if (typeof message.value == 'string') {
        const pinData = JSON.parse(message.value);
        pinBoard.push(pinData);
        io.emit('append-to-list', pinData)
    } else
        throw message.value;
});
```

The preceding code pulls the messages using the `consumer.on('message', function(message) {})` `event listener` method, and parses the messages using `JSON.parse` as the data recieved is stringified. As our JSON structure is same as that of the pins in the *pinBoard* app, we are going to emit the `pinData` to the `append-to-list Socket.IO` channel. This action was performed so that we can observe new pins in the browser after every minute.

4. Let's start the consumer node service by running the following command:

   node app.js

5. Then, let's connect to `http://localhost:3400/`:

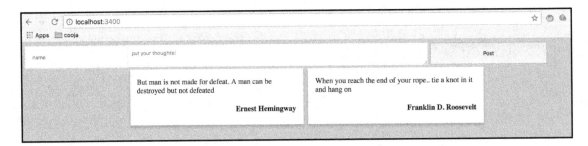

In the preceding output, we can see that a new thought will be added to the list every minute.

Note that we can connect as many consumer application to Kafka client running on different ports to receive Kafka messages from producer. Also, the producers can be scaled as consumers with respect to Kafka clusters. The only thing is to sustain cost of maintainability and then leverage the power of Kafka!

Summary

In this chapter, we implemented JSON data for real-time systems as well as distributed systems. The real-time implementation provides an overall idea of how data can be passed as collection with respect to WebSocket channels. The WebSocket implemented in `Socket.IO` is really fast and has worked reliably well. It is currently serving many application at the product level, such as Trello, Blog Talk Radio, and Zendesk.

Also, we learned about the concepts of distributed systems and implemented a small functionality in Kafka. The implementation of Kafka with an already-created real-time app yields ideas of scaling the real-time application that works like consumers.

Learning about the concepts of real-time and distributed systems prepares our readers to provide solutions for data availability and system scalability. In next chapter, we are going to learn about advanced JSON formats for implementing JSON data in various domains, such as geo-spatial domains, SEO, and data storage.

Case Studies in JSON 12

The JavaScript simple object notation was a seed for making a difference in the data exchange technologies domain. With its simple parenthesis {} format, key-value pair structure, readability, and ease of operations, has so much traction. JSON has become a pioneer in its field, on which other data exchange formats base themselves. There are various JSON formats available in the open source ecosystem, all of which are derived from JSON.

This chapter helps us to study those formats so that we can use them for various purposes. Here is list of formats we are going to focus on.

- GeoJSON
- JSONLD
- BSON
- MessagePack

Let's get started!

GeoJSON – a geospatial JSON data format

GeoJSON is a JSON-based implementation especially designed for the purpose of geospatial data. But wait—what do we mean by geospatial data? Geospatial data is information that represents a region of any space or its geometry.

Consider a random area next door to your house. The shape of the area may be visualized as a square, rectangle, or any other polygon that has specific measurements, and may be located using latitude and longitude coordinates.

GeoJSON was standardized by the **Internet Engineering Task Force** (**IETF**) community. GeoJSON provides specifications for all kinds of geographical data. Let's look at the structure of a basic geoJSON:

```
{
    "type": "Polygon",
    "coordinates": [
        [
            [100,0],
            [101,0],
            [101,1],
            [100,1],
            [100,0]
        ]
    ]
}
```

In the preceding JSON data, we have two keys. The type represents the geometry type, which refers to seven case-sensitive strings: `Point`, `MultiPoint`, `LineString`, `MultiLineString`, `Polygon`, `MultiPolygon`, and `GeometryCollection`.

Next is the coordinates key, which is list of array points for lat, long value pairs. Each pair of points comes together to form a geometric shape for the geometry type.

Every geometry object is wrapper for a `Feature` object. A `Feature` object comprises geometry and properties that a user can set as a JSON, or as null, or whatever else may be required. This can be presented as follows:

```
{
    "type": "Feature",
    "geometry":
    {
        "type": "LineString",
        "coordinates": [
            [102, 0],
            [103, 1],
            [104, 0],
            [105, 1]
        ]
    },
    "properties":
    {
        "prop0": "value0",
        "prop1": 0
    }
}
```

When an application requires multiple `Feature` lists, geoJSON also has an array structure arrangement called `featureCollection`. `featureCollection` consists of multiple features.

This media type can be applied for various fields, such as web mapping, geospatial databases, geographic data processing APIs, data analysis and storage services, and data dissemination.

Various tools available in the market that are based on geoJSON include `leaflet.js` (`http://leafletjs.com`), `cartodb` (`https://github.com/CartoDB/cartodb`), and `turf.js` (`http://turfjs.org/`).

JSONLD – a JSON format for SEO

JSONLD stands for **JSON with linked data structure**. First of all, let's understand what a linked data structure is. Say we are writing a new blog on block chains. While doing so, we would need to provide some metadata to our web crawler, assuming they are Google crawlers. The crawlers can parse our html and read the content of our blog. Now, this type of crawling is done by machine-reading methods rather than manually. Such input metadata may consist of some information that is linked with the next or previous blog post, or may be linked to the person who posted the blog. JSONLD provides a way to accomplish both. It works as a metadata for crawler as well as giving an idea about the links to other sets of data.

The Google search engine uses the crawled data to provide the best search results when someone searches for block chains.

JSONLD is used to connect data on the web. Let's understand the structure of JSONLD and its working with respect to linked data.

In web development, JSONLD is defined by `type="application/ld+json"` in the html `script` tag, as follows:

```
<script type="application/ld+json">
 {JSONLD data}
</script>
```

Unless you pass JSONLD within the `script` tag with type `application/ld+json`, it won't be recognized by the search engines.

Once our `script` tag is ready, we need to assign JSON-linked data to our context. We need to define the context of our JSON data. The context is anything that provides some background vocabulary to an entity. If our entity is an author, then the background vocabulary can include name, place, books, publication, and so on. Let's define our context as follows:

```
<script type="application/ld+json">
{
 "@context": "http://schema.org/Person"
}
</script>
```

In the preceding `script` tag, the context is linked with `schema.org` and specifically to a person entity. Let's find out what `schema.org` is:

> *Schema.org is a collaborative, community activity with a mission to create, maintain, and promote schemas for structured data on the Internet, on web pages, in email messages, and beyond.*

> *– schema.org*

If any site provides such structured data with respect to context, we can use one. One more such example is `https://json-ld.org/contexts/person.jsonld`.

The next important key is called `@type`. In our case, we have directly specified it in our `@context`, which is `person`. We can define it individually using the `@type` keyword. This can be done as follows:

```
<script type="application/ld+json">
{
    "@context": "http: //schema.org",
        "@type": "person",
    "name": "robin sharma",
    "work": {"
        @type": "CreativeWork",
        "About": "books,
        public speaking"
    }
}
</script>
```

The purpose of defining it differently is so that you can use a context for multiple types. In this case, to define our data regarding the person, we used `@type`. The types provides more properties, such as name and place. All the properties, such as name and about, are with respect to their `@type`.

Even though JSONLD has been available for a while, many websites do not take advantage of it. JSONLD is really important for SEO purposes, and needs to be considered to get the best SEO results.

BSON – a fast-traversal JSON format

We have already learned about BSON implementation in MongoDB. In fact, MongoDB was the first one to leverage BSON fully. We won't learn about other implementations for now, as they are beyond the scope of this book. Interested readers can visit this link for more information: `http://bsonspec.org/implementations.html`.

As JSON data is converted to binary, there is increase in the speed of traversal of BSON data. BSON extends the JSON data type collection by providing more data type support with respect to binData and Date type. These advantages make BSON capable of using it as a record for any unstructured database design.

If the BSON format is used for data passing over network, as the data is binary, the encoding and decoding of data among different network devices is simpler and can be done at quicker speeds.

BSON is storage efficient—still, it may be slightly bigger in size when compared to serialized JSON. This is because BSON data has more properties, such as date types and data lengths, present for data.

Better compressions with messagePack

There is one more data exchange format which is more space efficient than all those that we've covered so far. It provides binary serialization and is designed for fast in-memory manipulations. Many renowned sites, such as Pinterest, use messagePack for the compression of data.

Consider a scenario where we have to cache some data in primary cache storage, such as redis. In such a case, everytime a developer needs to store data—which can be JSON, an array, or any other data type—into a single string associated with a key (as in redis, where the data store is key-value pair with single-level depth), the memory utilization increases relative to the data inserted. messagePack can help to reduce the memory utilization. If we encode data using messagePack, it results in around 40% lossless compression. Isn't that better?

Another application, as suggested by the author of messagePack, is the cross-service RPC communication protocol. This could be a scenario where two different application processes want to communicate for a purpose, and the data passed across the processes may require some extra overhead implementation while processing and storage referred as Endianness. You can use messagePack as a common communication protocol for RPC.

 messagePack is not so fast when compared with a normal JSON parser that runs on Google's v8 compiler. v8 provides high optimization with C++ string marshaling. Someone has benchmarked the messagePack library with a JSON encoder on v8 engine; here are the results: `https://github.com/mattheworiordan/nodejs-encoding-benchmarks`.

Summary

In this chapter, we learned about some JSON format case studies. Each case has its own advantages and implications, which every reader needs to be aware of while making a rational decision for its implementation. And that's all, folks! I hope you have had a great time learning all the JSON essentials in the book and enjoyed the learning curves. This is not the end—the journey begins right now! Start small and practice constantly, because the cumulative effort matters than just the mere motivation for doing anything.

Other Books You May Enjoy

If you enjoyed this book, you may be interested in these other books by Packt:

Hands-On Data Structures and Algorithms with JavaScript
Kashyap Mukkamala

ISBN: 978-1-78839-855-8

- Build custom Back buttons embedded within your application
- Build part of a basic JavaScript syntax parser and evaluator for an online IDE
- Build a custom activity user tracker for your application
- Generate accurate recommendations for credit card approval using Decision Trees
- Simplify complex problems using a graphs
- Increase the performance of an application using micro-optimizations

Mastering JavaScript Functional Programming
Federico Kereki

ISBN: 978-1-78728-744-0

- Create more reliable code with closures and immutable data
- Convert existing methods into pure functions, and loops into recursive methods
- Develop more powerful applications with currying and function composition
- Separate the logic of your system from implementation details
- Implement composition and chaining techniques to simplify coding
- Use functional programming techniques where it makes the most sense

Leave a review - let other readers know what you think

Please share your thoughts on this book with others by leaving a review on the site that you bought it from. If you purchased the book from Amazon, please leave us an honest review on this book's Amazon page. This is vital so that other potential readers can see and use your unbiased opinion to make purchasing decisions, we can understand what our customers think about our products, and our authors can see your feedback on the title that they have worked with Packt to create. It will only take a few minutes of your time, but is valuable to other potential customers, our authors, and Packt. Thank you!

Index

CPSIA information can be obtained
at www.ICGtesting.com
Printed in the USA
FSHW02n2038100518
48115FS